GW00359947

PRACTICE NOT

THE AUDIT OF INSURERS IN THE UNITED KINGDOM (Revised)

(Effective for periods ending on or after 15 December 2010)

Contents	*Page*

Preface	3
Introduction	4
Legislative and Regulatory Framework	5
The audit of financial statements	
ISAs (UK and Ireland)	14
200 Overall Objectives of the Independent Auditor and the Conduct of an Audit in Accordance with International Standards on Auditing (UK and Ireland)	14
210 Agreeing the Terms of Audit Engagements	16
220 Quality Control for an Audit of Financial Statements	19
230 Audit Documentation	21
240 The Auditor's Responsibilities Relating to Fraud in an Audit of Financial Statements	22
250 Section A – Consideration of Laws and Regulations in an Audit of Financial Statements	26
250 Section B – The Auditor's Right and Duty to Report to Regulators in the Financial Sector	31
300 Planning an Audit of Financial Statements	42
315 Identifying and Assessing the Risks of Material Misstatement Through Understanding the Entity and its Environment	45
320 Materiality in Planning and Performing an Audit	55
330 The Auditor's Responses to Assessed Risks	58
402 Audit Considerations Relating to an Entity Using a Service Organization	63
450 Evaluation of Misstatements Identified During the Audit	66
500 Audit Evidence	68
505 External Confirmations	69
520 Analytical Procedures	71

540 Auditing Accounting Estimates, Including Fair Value Accounting
Estimates and Related Disclosures   73

550 Related Parties   85

560 Subsequent Events   87

570 Going Concern   89

580 Written Representations   91

600 Special Considerations – Audits of Group Financial Statements (Including
the Work of Component Auditors)   93

620 Using the Work of an Auditor's Expert   96

700 The Auditor's Report on Financial Statements   99

705 Modifications to Opinions in the Independent Auditor's Report   105

706 Emphasis of Matter Paragraphs and Other Matter Paragraphs in the
Independent Auditor's Report   107

720 Section A – The Auditor's Responsibilities Relating to Other Information in
Documents Containing Audited Financial Statements   109

Reporting on regulatory returns   111

Appendices   131

Appendix 1   Illustrative examples of auditor's reports

Reports on regulatory returns

1.1 Composite insurer   132

1.2 Life insurer   135

1.3 General insurer   138

1.4 Statement on the group capital adequacy report   140

Reports relating to a Lloyd's syndicate

1.5 Personal accounts and syndicate MAPA accounts   142

Other reports by the auditor

1.6 Report on interim net profits   144

Appendix 2   The main parts of FSMA 2000 relevant to insurers   145

Appendix 3   The FSA Handbook   147

Appendix 4   Reporting direct to FSA – statutory right and protection for
disclosure under general law   151

Appendix 5   Definitions   153

Appendix 6   Cross references to significant topics dealt with in the Practice Note   158

PREFACE

This Practice Note contains guidance on the application of auditing standards issued by the Auditing Practices Board (APB) to the audit of insurers in the United Kingdom. It also contains guidance on auditor's reports in connection with regulatory returns and the auditor's duty to report to the Financial Services Authority (FSA) and to the Council of Lloyd's.

This Practice Note is supplementary to, and should be read in conjunction with, the International Standards on Auditing (ISAs) (UK and Ireland) that apply to audits of financial statements for periods ending on or after 15 December 2010. This Practice Note sets out the special considerations relating to the audit of insurers which arise from individual ISAs (UK and Ireland) listed in the contents. It is not the intention of the Practice Note to provide step-by-step guidance to the audit of insurers, so where no special considerations arise from a particular ISA (UK and Ireland), no material is included.

The guidance in this Practice Note is applicable to auditors of insurance companies and of Lloyd's syndicates and corporate members. Particular considerations relating to Lloyd's syndicates are generally shown at the end of each section of text and, to assist clarity, are presented with a blue background.

The following Practice Notes issued by the APB are also relevant to the audit of insurers:

PN 12 (Revised)   Money Laundering – Guidance for auditors on UK legislation

PN 16 (Revised)   Bank reports for audit purposes in the United Kingdom

PN 22   The Auditors' Consideration of FRS 17 "Retirement Benefits" – Defined Benefit Schemes

PN 23 (Revised)   Auditing Complex Financial Instruments – Interim Guidance

This Practice Note has been prepared with advice and assistance from staff of the FSA (in so far as the obligations of an insurer and its auditor under the FSA Handbook are concerned) and of Lloyd's. It is based on the legislation, regulations and byelaws which were in effect at 31 October 2010. The Practice Note does not, however, constitute general guidance given by the FSA or Lloyd's or Industry Guidance. It is not an exhaustive list of all the obligations that an insurer and its auditor may have under the Financial Services and Markets Act 2000 (FSMA 2000), the FSA Handbook or Lloyd's byelaws.

INTRODUCTION

1. The term "insurers" in this Practice Note should be taken to refer to the following types of entity:-

    (a) UK insurance companies authorised by the FSA[1];

    (b) Lloyd's syndicates and corporate members; and

    (c) Overseas insurers with UK branches.

2. This Practice Note addresses the responsibilities and obligations of the auditor concerning:

    - The audit of the insurer's financial statements, as required by sections 495 and 496 of the Companies Act 2006 (CA 2006) and in relation to Lloyd's the 2008 Regulations[2] and the Syndicate Accounting Byelaw[3].

    - Reporting on parts of the insurer's regulatory returns, as required by rule 9.35 of IPRU(INS), and in relation to Lloyd's the Solvency and Reporting Byelaw (No. 5 of 2007) (the "Solvency Byelaw"). Guidance on the auditor's work in relation to such returns is set out in the section of this Practice Note dealing with regulatory returns.

    - Where applicable reporting on the insurer's group capital adequacy report, as required by rule 9.40(3)(c) of IPRU(INS). Guidance on the auditor's work in relation to such reports is set out in the section of this Practice Note dealing with group capital adequacy.

    - The right and duty to report direct to the FSA[4] (and, where appropriate, to Lloyd's) in certain circumstances.

    - Reporting on interim profits for the purposes of their inclusion in capital resources.

3. Overseas insurers operating in the UK through branches are not subject to the audit provisions of CA 2006 and so the terms of engagement are a matter of contract between the auditor and its client who may, for example, be local or head office management or the insurer's home country auditor.

---

1   Guidance relating to Friendly Societies is set out in PN 24 "The audit of friendly societies in the United Kingdom (Revised)".
2   Statutory Instrument SI 2008 No. 1950 "The Insurance Accounts Directive (Lloyd's Syndicate and Aggregate Accounts) Regulations 2008".
3   Auditors of Lloyd's syndicates are required to be "recognised accountants", that is, registered auditors who have been approved by Lloyd's and have given an undertaking to the Council of Lloyd's in a prescribed form.
4   Statutory Instrument SI 2001 No. 2587 "The FSMA 2000 (Communications by Auditors) Regulations 2001 and sections 342 and 343 of FSMA 2000".

4.   Such engagements take many different forms: the auditor may be asked to report on the financial statements of the UK branch or only on particular aspects thereof, and the form of its opinion will also vary from case to case. The auditor undertaking such assignments may wish to consider the guidance in this Practice Note where relevant, having regard to the agreed scope of its engagement.

LEGISLATIVE AND REGULATORY FRAMEWORK

Background

5.   Insurers operate within a complex framework of law and regulation which differs in a number of significant respects from that applicable to the generality of commercial enterprises. This framework involves regulation of insurance activities established by European Directive, under which insurance regulators have powers to establish specific requirements as well as to institute investigations into insurers and to suspend or remove authorisation to conduct insurance business where appropriate. For the purpose of this Practice Note, references to the auditor of a regulated entity or an authorised person in the context of FSA prudential supervision of insurers includes the auditor of a Lloyd's syndicate or corporate member, unless otherwise stated.

6.   Insurance business may not be carried on in the United Kingdom without authorisation to do so. Insurance may be undertaken by:

(a) Companies holding permission under Part IV of FSMA 2000 to carry on the regulated activities of effecting and/or carrying out contracts of insurance (companies incorporated under CA 2006 and companies with their head offices outside the EU);

(b) Members of Lloyd's (see Section 316 of FSMA 2000); and

(c) Insurers authorised by other EEA member states which may conduct insurance business in the UK on a "freedom to provide services" basis or through the establishment of branches and which qualify automatically for authorisation under FSMA 2000.

In the case of members of Lloyd's, the FSA applies requirements and reporting obligations at the level of the market as a whole and on managing agents.

7.   As well as needing permission under Part IV of FSMA 2000 to effect or carry out contracts of insurance, an insurer is likely to require additional permissions in respect of its activities relating to marketing, arranging or advising on insurance contracts and to dealing in investments as principal where it uses derivatives as part of its investment policy. Life insurers are likely to require further permissions as many life policies are deemed to represent designated investment business[5].

---

5   Further guidance in connection with insurance intermediaries is included in ICAEW TECH 1/06: *Interim guidance for auditors of insurance intermediaries on client asset reporting requirements.*

8.   The principal objective of insurance regulation is to provide appropriate protection to policyholders. The specific regulatory objectives of the FSA are described in paragraph 28 below.

9.   Requirements concerning the auditor's duty to report are set out in Statutory Instrument SI 2001 No 2587 "The FSMA 2000 (Communications by Auditors) Regulations 2001" (the 2001 Regulations). Guidance on the auditor's duty to report to the FSA (and, where relevant, to Lloyd's) in the context of current legislation is set out in the section on ISA (UK and Ireland) 250 Section B in this Practice Note.

10. An insurer carrying on long-term insurance business is required by SUP 4.3.1R(1)(a) to appoint an actuary to perform the actuarial function. The holder of this function is required, among other things, to advise the entity's governing body on the methods and assumptions to be used for the actuarial investigation, and to carry out that investigation in accordance with the methods and assumptions decided upon by the governing body. The purpose of the investigation, which is required once in every period of twelve months and at any other time when there is to be a distribution of surplus from the long-term fund, is:

     (a) To value the liabilities attributable to long-term business; and

     (b) To determine any excess over those liabilities of the assets representing the long-term business fund.

11. An insurer which writes with-profits business is also required by SUP 4.3.1R(1)(b) to appoint an actuary to perform the with-profits actuary function. This actuary is required by SUP 4.3.16AR, among other things, to advise a firm's management at the appropriate level of seniority on key aspects of the discretion to be exercised in respect of with-profits business.

12. A significant part of the FSA's regulatory framework consists of provisions intended to maintain the solvency of insurers and so ensure their ability to meet future claims from policyholders. Accordingly, insurers are required to comply with solvency requirements and also to submit annual regulatory returns providing information concerning the value and type of assets held, claims arising under policies written and other financial information. These annual returns are public documents.

13. The auditor of an insurer needs to be familiar with the relevant legal and regulatory requirements. The extent to which an auditor considers compliance with regulatory requirements in the course of auditing an insurer's financial statements is discussed in the section of this Practice Note that addresses ISA (UK and Ireland) 250 Section B. Guidance on auditor's responsibilities in relation to regulatory reporting is contained in the "Reporting on regulatory returns" section of this Practice Note.

14. Aspects of the legislative and regulatory framework that are considered in the remainder of this section are:

- Financial statements.

- Financial Services and Markets Act 2000.

- Prudential requirements.

- Reporting direct to the FSA – statutory right and duty.

- Communication between the FSA and the auditor.

Additional Considerations relating to Lloyd's

15. The FSA oversees Lloyd's regulation to ensure consistency with general standards in financial services. Much of the Lloyd's market rule structure is embedded in a series of byelaws passed by the Council. Changes to regulatory requirements are communicated to the market by means of market bulletins.

16. Members underwrite insurance business at Lloyd's as a member of one or more syndicates, each syndicate being managed by a managing agent. Syndicates have no legal personality and are merely the vehicle through which the members underwrite insurance risk. Technically, each syndicate is an annual venture. The year during which it writes business is described as an "underwriting year" or a "year of account". Members have no liability for business underwritten by the same syndicate in previous years of account unless they were members in those years or unless they have reinsured the members of that syndicate for the previous years. However, for practical business purposes, syndicates are treated as continuing from one year to the next. Lloyd's maintains central assets, including the Central Fund, which are available to meet a member's underwriting liabilities in the event of any default by the member.

17. Arrangements for conducting business at Lloyd's involve requirements for trust funds to be maintained in accordance with various trust deeds, some of which confer various powers and authorities on managing agents.

18. FSA rules require the involvement of an actuary to express an opinion on the general insurance business solvency technical provisions and to determine the life business solvency technical provisions.

19. Lloyd's corporate members are not regulated by the FSA. They are subject to Lloyd's requirements. Each Lloyd's corporate member is required to maintain appropriate assets at Lloyd's or other security in favour of Lloyd's to support insurance underwritten on its behalf at Lloyd's.

Financial statements

20. The form and content of the financial statements of UK insurers prepared under UK GAAP is governed by CA 2006 and United Kingdom Accounting Standards. (United Kingdom Accounting Standards comprise: Statements of Standard Accounting Practice ("SSAPs"), Financial Reporting Standards ("FRSs") and UITF Abstracts.) The prescribed format for a UK insurer's financial statements that comply with UK GAAP is set out in:

(a) Sections 395 and 396 of CA 2006; and

(b) Schedules 3 and 6 (part 3) to The Large and Medium-sized Companies and Groups (Accounts and Reports) Regulations 2008 (SI 2008/410) (The 2008 Accounts and Reports Regulations).

In addition, financial statements of insurance companies prepared under UK GAAP are expected to be prepared in accordance with the guidance in the Statement of Recommended Practice "Accounting for insurance business" issued by the Association of British Insurers (ABI), (the Insurance SORP). However, listed UK groups (including listed UK insurance groups) must prepare consolidated financial statements in accordance with International Financial Reporting Standards as adopted by the European Union (EU-IFRSs)[6] and those parts of CA 2006 applicable to companies reporting under EU-IFRSs. UK companies or non listed groups, including UK insurers and insurance groups, are permitted to voluntarily adopt EU-IFRSs for their financial statements.

21. If an authorised insurer preparing financial statements under UK GAAP undertakes long-term business, computation of the technical provision for long-term business to be included in its financial statements must be made by a Fellow of the Institute and Faculty of Actuaries based on recognised actuarial methods with due regard to the actuarial principles laid down in Directive 2002/83/EC of the European Parliament and of the Council concerning life insurance. This requirement does not apply to any other technical provisions of the insurer or, directly, to the technical provisions shown in the financial statements of a Lloyd's corporate member. The actuary carrying out the computation (known as "the Reporting Actuary") may, but is not required to, make a report in the financial statements relating to the provision.

Additional considerations relating to Lloyd's

22. The reporting requirements in respect of syndicate activities are set out in "The Insurance Accounts Directive (Lloyd's Syndicate and Aggregate Accounts) Regulations 2008" ("the 2008 Lloyd's Regulations"). The 2008 Lloyd's Regulations require the preparation by managing agents of:

---

6   Article 4 of EC Regulation 1606/2002 as acknowledged in section 403(1) CA 2006 – the IAS Regulation.

(a) Syndicate annual accounts in accordance with CA 2006 and Schedule 3 to The 2008 Accounts and Reports Regulations showing the performance across all years of account of the syndicate during the calendar year;

(b) Syndicate underwriting year accounts at the closure of a year of account (unless all the relevant members of the syndicate agree otherwise); and by the Council of Lloyd's

(c) Aggregate accounts for the Lloyd's market as a whole reflecting an accumulation of the syndicate profit and loss accounts and the balance sheets prepared at (a).

In addition, the Syndicate Accounting Byelaw 2005 requires the preparation by managing agents of syndicate underwriting year accounts at 31 December each year in respect of each run-off account (unless all the relevant members of the syndicate agree otherwise).

23. The requirements for the minimum form and content of syndicate underwriting year accounts (referred to at paragraph 22(b) above), together with other related financial reporting requirements, are set out in the Syndicate Accounting Byelaw 2005. The syndicate annual accounts (referred to at paragraph 22(a) above), must be prepared in accordance with UK GAAP on an earned basis of recognition.

24. Legally, each year of account of a syndicate is a separate venture established to write insurance business in a specific calendar year. As a consequence of each annual venture being a unique trading entity, a mechanism is necessary to enable each such venture to close, normally at the end of three years. Estimated outstanding liabilities as at the date of closure are reinsured, in consideration for a premium, by a subsequent year of account of the same or another syndicate. This reinsurance arrangement is known as a "reinsurance to close" ("RITC").

25. In certain circumstances, the managing agent may conclude that significant uncertainties (or other factors) exist such that it is not possible to determine an appropriate premium for a RITC at the normal date of closure. When this happens, the relevant year of account is not closed but placed into run-off until such time as the managing agent concludes that this requirement can be satisfied. Technical provisions will be determined for each run-off account and carried forward until the year of account is closed or all its liabilities discharged.

26. Where the Lloyd's corporate member is a UK company it is required to prepare its financial statements in accordance with the requirements of CA 2006 applicable to UK insurance companies whether drawn up in accordance with EU-IFRSs or UK GAAP.

Financial Services and Markets Act 2000

27.   FSMA 2000 sets out the high level regulatory framework for the financial sector more generally and not just insurers. Appendix 2 sets out the main parts of FSMA 2000 relevant to authorised firms[7] which are insurers.

28.   The wide scope of FSMA 2000 reflects the FSA's extensive responsibilities. These are set out in FSMA 2000 as regulatory objectives covering:

(a) Market confidence;

(b) Public awareness;

(c) Financial stability;

(d) The protection of consumers; and

(e) The reduction of financial crime.

29.   FSMA 2000 covers not only the regulation and supervision of financial sector entities but also other issues such as official listing rules, business transfers, market abuse, compensation and ombudsman schemes, investment exchanges and clearing houses. FSMA 2000 is also supported by a large number of statutory instruments. Significant components of the definition and scope of the regulatory framework are contained in the main statutory instruments.

30.   Under Part X FSMA 2000 the FSA has the power to make "rules" and give guidance. The legal effect of a rule varies depending on the power under which it is made and on the language used in the rule. Rules are mandatory unless a waiver has been agreed with the FSA. If an authorised firm contravenes a rule it may be subject to enforcement action and consequent disciplinary measures under Part XIV FSMA 2000. Furthermore, in certain circumstances an authorised firm may be subject to an action for damages under section 150 FSMA 2000. In contrast, guidance is generally issued to throw light on a particular aspect of regulatory requirements, and is not binding. However if an authorised firm acts in accordance with it in the circumstances contemplated by that guidance, the FSA will proceed on the basis that the authorised firm has complied with the rule to which the guidance relates.

31.   Rules made by the FSA and associated general guidance are set out in the FSA Handbook of Rules and Guidance ("the FSA Handbook") (see Appendix 3). The main FSA systems and control requirements are set out in the Senior management arrangements, systems and controls element of the high level standards block of the FSA Handbook ("SYSC").

---

7   An entity which has been granted one or more Part IV permissions by the FSA and so is authorised under FSMA 2000 to undertake regulated activities.

32.   It is clearly unrealistic to expect all members of an audit engagement team to have detailed knowledge of the entire FSA Handbook; rather ISA (UK and Ireland) 250 Section B requires the level of knowledge to be appropriate to the staff member's role in the audit and sufficient (in the context of that role) to enable them to identify situations which may give reasonable cause to believe that a matter should be reported to the FSA[8]. ISA (UK and Ireland) 220 requires the engagement partner, among other things, to:

- Take responsibility for the engagement team undertaking appropriate consultation on difficult or contentious matters.

- Be satisfied that members of the engagement team have undertaken appropriate consultation during the course of the engagement, both within the engagement team and between the engagement team and others at the appropriate level within or outside the firm[9].

Prudential requirements

33.   Insurers are subject to certain prudential requirements which are detailed in IPRU(INS)[10], which set out the reporting requirements, certain of the rules relating to long-term insurance business and various definitions, and GENPRU[11], INSPRU[12] and SYSC[13], which set out the rules and guidance on the assessment of risk, capital requirements and capital resources.

34.   A significant part of the FSA's regulatory framework consists of provisions intended to maintain the solvency of insurers and so ensure their ability to meet future claims from policyholders. An insurer must maintain capital resources equal to or in excess of its capital resources requirement at all times. In order to monitor solvency and assess other risks and exposures, insurers are required to submit returns to the FSA providing:

(a)   Information concerning the value and type of assets held, claims arising under policies written and other financial information;

(b)   The determination of the Individual Capital Assessment (an unaudited calculation not available for public inspection); and

(c)   Where applicable, the group capital adequacy calculation.

---

8   ISA (UK and Ireland) 250 Section B paragraph 11.
9   ISA (UK and Ireland) 220 paragraph 18.
10   Interim Prudential Sourcebook for Insurers.
11   General Prudential Sourcebook.
12   Prudential Sourcebook for Insurers.
13   Senior Management Arrangements, Systems and Controls.

Reporting direct to the FSA – statutory right and duty

35. Under the 2001 Regulations the auditor of an authorised firm or the auditor of an entity closely linked to an authorised firm who is also the auditor of that authorised firm has a statutory duty to communicate matters of material significance to the FSA. Under section 340 FSMA 2000 "the auditor" is defined as one required to be appointed under FSA "rules" or appointed as a result of another enactment. In addition section 342 FSMA 2000 provides that no duty to which the auditor is subject shall be contravened by communicating in good faith to the FSA any information or opinion on a matter that the auditor reasonably believes is relevant to any functions of the FSA. There is a similar right and duty of the auditor of a Lloyd's syndicate or corporate member to report direct to Lloyd's by the undertaking required from the auditor of a Lloyd's syndicate or corporate member by the Lloyd's Audit Arrangements Byelaw 1998 and the Lloyd's Membership Byelaw No 5 of 2005. These duties do not require the auditor of an insurer to undertake additional work directed at identifying matters to report over and above the work necessary to fulfil its obligations to report on financial statements and regulatory returns. Guidance on the identification of matters to be reported to the regulators is set out in the section dealing with ISA (UK and Ireland) 250 Section B.

Communication between the FSA and the auditor

36. Within the legal constraints that apply, the FSA may pass on to the auditor any information which it considers relevant to its function. The auditor is bound by the confidentiality provisions set out in Regulations made under Part XXIII of FSMA 2000 (Public record, disclosure of information and co-operation) in respect of confidential information received from the FSA. An auditor may not pass on such confidential information, even to the entity being audited, without lawful authority (for example, if an exception applies under FSMA 2000 (Disclosure of Confidential Information) Regulations 2001) or without the consent of the person from whom the information was received and, if different, to whom the information relates.

37. Before communicating to an authorised firm any information received from the FSA, the auditor considers carefully whether:

(a) The auditor has received the FSA's express permission to communicate a particular item of information;

(b) The information relates to any other party whose permission may need to be obtained before disclosure can be made; and

(c) The information was received by FSA in a capacity other than discharging its functions under FSMA 2000 or from another regulator (in which case the auditor may either be prohibited from disclosure or may need permission of the party which provided the information to that regulator).

The auditor may however disclose to an authorised firm information it has communicated to the FSA except where to do so would have the effect of disclosing information communicated to it by the FSA. If there is any doubt the auditor considers the matters above.

38. Matters communicated by the FSA during any bilateral meeting may be conveyed by those representatives of the auditor who were present at the meeting (or otherwise received the communication directly) to other partners, directors and employees of the auditor who need to know the information in connection with the auditor's performance of its duties relating to that authorised firm without the FSA's express permission. However, in the interests of prudence and transparency the auditor informs the FSA that it will be discussing the issues covered with colleagues.

39. Where the FSA passes to the auditor information which it considers is relevant to the auditor's function, the auditor considers its implications in the context of its work and may need to amend its approach accordingly. However, the fact that the auditor may have been informed of such a matter by the regulator does not, of itself, require the auditor to change the scope of the work, nor does it necessarily require it actively to search for evidence in support of the situation communicated by the regulator.

40. The auditor is required to cooperate with the FSA (SUP 3.8.2R). This may involve attending meetings and providing the FSA with information about the authorised firm that the FSA may reasonably request in discharging its functions. For example this can arise in relation to FSA ARROW II risk assessments.

41. The auditor must notify the FSA without delay if the auditor is removed from office, resigns before the term of office expires or is not reappointed by the authorised firm. Notification to the FSA includes communicating any matters connected with this event that the auditor considers ought to be drawn to the FSA's attention or a statement that there are no such matters (section 344 FSMA 2000 and SUP 3.8.11R and 12R).

THE AUDIT OF FINANCIAL STATEMENTS

This Practice Note contains guidance on the application to the audits of financial statements of insurers of those ISAs (UK and Ireland) that are effective for periods ending on or after 15 December 2010. The purpose of the following paragraphs is to identify the special considerations arising from the application of the "Requirements" of ISAs (UK and Ireland) to the audit of insurers, and to suggest ways in which these can be addressed (extracts from ISAs (UK and Ireland) are indicated by grey-shaded boxes below). This Practice Note does not contain commentary on all of the requirements included in the ISAs (UK and Ireland) and reading it should not be seen as an alternative to reading the relevant ISAs (UK and Ireland) in their entirety. In addition, where no special considerations arise from a particular ISA (UK and Ireland), no material is included.

ISA (UK AND IRELAND) 200: OVERALL OBJECTIVES OF THE INDEPENDENT AUDITOR AND THE CONDUCT OF AN AUDIT IN ACCORDANCE WITH INTERNATIONAL STANDARDS ON AUDITING (UK AND IRELAND)

Scope of this ISA (UK and Ireland)
This International Standard on Auditing (UK and Ireland) (ISA (UK and Ireland)) deals with the independent auditor's overall responsibilities when conducting an audit of financial statements in accordance with ISAs (UK and Ireland). Specifically, it sets out the overall objectives of the independent auditor, and explains the nature and scope of an audit designed to enable the independent auditor to meet those objectives. It also explains the scope, authority and structure of the ISAs (UK and Ireland), and includes requirements establishing the general responsibilities of the independent auditor applicable in all audits, including the obligation to comply with the ISAs (UK and Ireland). The independent auditor is referred to as "the auditor" hereafter. (paragraph 1)

Overall Objectives of the Auditor
In conducting an audit of financial statements, the overall objectives of the auditor are:

(a) To obtain reasonable assurance about whether the financial statements as a whole are free from material misstatement, whether due to fraud or error, thereby enabling the auditor to express an opinion on whether the financial statements are prepared, in all material respects, in accordance with an applicable financial reporting framework; and

(b) To report on the financial statements, and communicate as required by the ISAs (UK and Ireland), in accordance with the auditor's findings. (paragraph 11)

In all cases when reasonable assurance cannot be obtained and a qualified opinion in the auditor's report is insufficient in the circumstances for purposes of reporting to the intended users of the financial statements, the ISAs (UK and Ireland) require that the auditor disclaim an opinion or withdraw from the engagement, where withdrawal is possible under applicable law or regulation. (paragraph 12)

The auditor shall comply with relevant ethical requirements, including those pertaining to independence, relating to financial statement audit engagements. (paragraph 14)

The auditor shall plan and perform an audit with professional skepticism, recognizing that circumstances may exist that cause the financial statements to be materially misstated. (paragraph 15)

42.   The auditor should comply with the APB's Ethical Standards for Auditors and relevant ethical guidance relating to the work of auditors issued by the auditor's professional body. A fundamental principle is that the auditor should not accept or perform work which it is not competent to undertake. The importance of technical competence is also underlined in the Auditors' Code[14], issued by the APB, which states that the necessary degree of professional skill demands an understanding of financial reporting and business issues, together with expertise in accumulating and assessing the evidence necessary to form an opinion. An auditor should not undertake the audit of an insurer unless it is satisfied that it has, or can obtain, the necessary level of competence.

Independence

43.   Independence issues can be complex for the auditor of an insurer because of insurance contracts that the auditor or its partners and staff may have with the insurer. Independence is addressed in the APB's Ethical Standard for Auditors 2 (Revised) – Financial, business, employment and personal relationships.

---

14   This is Appendix 2 of the APB's Scope and Authority of Pronouncements (Revised).

ISA (UK AND IRELAND) 210: AGREEING THE TERMS OF AUDIT ENGAGEMENTS

Objective

The objective of the auditor is to accept or continue an audit engagement only when the basis upon which it is to be performed has been agreed, through:

(a) Establishing whether the preconditions for an audit are present; and

(b) Confirming that there is a common understanding between the auditor and management and, where appropriate, those charged with governance of the terms of the audit engagement. (paragraph 3)

The auditor shall agree the terms of the audit engagement with those charged with governance. (paragraph 9)

Subject to paragraph 11, the agreed terms of the audit engagement shall be recorded in an audit engagement letter or other suitable form of written agreement and shall include:

(a) The objective and scope of the audit of the financial statements;

(b) The responsibilities of the auditor;

(c) The responsibilities of those charged with governance;

(d) Identification of the applicable financial reporting framework for the preparation of the financial statements; and

(e) Reference to the expected form and content of any reports to be issued by the auditor and a statement that there may be circumstances in which a report may differ from its expected form and content. (paragraph 10)

If law or regulation prescribes in sufficient detail the terms of the audit engagement referred to in paragraph 10, the auditor need not record them in a written agreement, except for the fact that such law or regulation applies and that management acknowledges and understands its responsibilities as set out in paragraph 6(b). (paragraph 11)

44. The auditor may choose to combine into a single letter the terms of engagement in relation to the audit of regulatory returns and the group capital adequacy return (if applicable). Matters which the auditor may decide to refer to in the engagement letter are as follows:

- The responsibility of the directors/senior management to comply with applicable FSMA 2000 legislation and FSA Handbook rules and guidance including the need to keep the FSA informed about the affairs of the entity.

- The statutory right and duty of the auditor to report direct to the FSA in certain circumstances (see the section of this Practice Note relating to ISA (UK and Ireland) 250 Section B).

- The requirement to cooperate with the auditor (SUP 3.6.1R). This includes taking steps to ensure that, where applicable, each of its appointed representatives and material outsourcers gives the auditor the same right of access to records, information and explanations as the authorised firm itself is required to provide the auditor (section 341 FSMA 2000 and SUP 3.6.2G to 3.6.8G). It is a criminal offence for an insurer or its officers, controllers or managers to provide false or misleading information to the auditor (section 346 FSMA 2000).

- The need for the insurer to make the auditor aware when it appoints a third party (including another department or office of the same audit firm) to review, investigate or report on any aspects of its business activities that may be relevant to the audit of the financial statements and to provide the auditor with copies of reports by such a third party promptly after their receipt.

45.   In this connection the auditor is aware that:

    (a) The FSA does not need to approve the appointment of an auditor but may seek to satisfy itself that an auditor appointed by a firm is independent and has the necessary skills, resources and experience (SUP 3.4.4G, 3.4.7R and 3.4.8G);

    (b) The auditor is required to cooperate with the FSA (SUP 3.8.2R); and

    (c) The auditor must notify the FSA if the auditor ceases to be the auditor of an authorised firm. (SUP 3.8.11R and 3.8.12R)

Additional considerations relating to Lloyd's

46.   Further matters specific to Lloyd's syndicates and Lloyd's corporate members which may be dealt with in the engagement letter include:

- The responsibilities of the directors of the managing agent or Lloyd's corporate member to keep Lloyd's informed about the affairs of these businesses.

- The auditor's additional duty to report matters to the Council of Lloyd's of which it has become aware in its capacity as auditor which may be of material significance to Lloyd's in its capacity as market supervisor.

- The auditor's duty to provide access to its working papers to the Council of Lloyd's in certain circumstances.

47. The engagement letter for a Lloyd's syndicate also refers to the aspects of the auditor's responsibilities, as set out in the Audit Arrangements Byelaw ("AAB"), as the syndicate's "recognised accountant", namely:

   (a) To report on the syndicate's financial statements and related matters;

   (b) To report on any syndicate Annual Return as required by or under the Solvency and Reporting Byelaw; and

   (c) As reporting accountant, if appointed by the Council of Lloyd's to report on other specified matters.

ISA (UK AND IRELAND) 220: QUALITY CONTROL FOR AN AUDIT OF FINANCIAL STATEMENTS

Objective

The objective of the auditor is to implement quality control procedures at the engagement level that provide the auditor with reasonable assurance that:

(a) The audit complies with professional standards and applicable legal and regulatory requirements; and

(b) The auditor's report issued is appropriate in the circumstances. (paragraph 6)

Quality control systems, policies and procedures are the responsibility of the audit firm. Under ISQC (UK and Ireland) 1, the firm has an obligation to establish and maintain a system of quality control to provide it with reasonable assurance that:

(a) The firm and its personnel comply with professional standards and applicable legal and regulatory requirements; and

(b) The reports issued by the firm or engagement partners are appropriate in the circumstances. (paragraph 2)

48. Quality control procedures cover the work of members of the engagement team with actuarial expertise or other specialist knowledge, and have regard to ISA (UK and Ireland) 620 "Using the Work of an Auditor's Expert" in relation to the involvement of external actuarial or other expertise.

The engagement partner shall be satisfied that the engagement team, and any auditor's experts who are not part of the engagement team, collectively have the appropriate competence and capabilities to:

(a) Perform the audit engagement in accordance with professional standards and applicable legal and regulatory requirements; and

(b) Enable an auditor's report that is appropriate in the circumstances to be issued. (paragraph 14)

49. As well as ensuring that the engagement team has an appropriate level of knowledge of the industry and its corresponding products, the engagement partner also satisfies himself that the members of the engagement team have sufficient knowledge of the

regulatory framework within which insurers operate commensurate with their roles on the engagement and that, where appropriate, the team includes members with actuarial expertise or has access to external actuarial expertise appropriate to the entity's insurance business.

ISA (UK AND IRELAND) 230: AUDIT DOCUMENTATION

Objective
The objective of the auditor is to prepare documentation that provides:

(a) A sufficient and appropriate record of the basis for the auditor's report; and

(b) Evidence that the audit was planned and performed in accordance with the ISAs (UK and Ireland) and applicable legal and regulatory requirements. (paragraph 5)

The auditor shall prepare audit documentation that is sufficient to enable an experienced auditor, having no previous connection with the audit, to understand:

(a) The nature, timing and extent of the audit procedures performed to comply with the ISAs (UK and Ireland) and applicable legal and regulatory requirements;

(b) The results of the audit procedures performed, and the audit evidence obtained; and

(c) Significant matters arising during the audit, the conclusions reached thereon, and significant professional judgments made in reaching those conclusions. (paragraph 8)

50. If the auditor uses in-house actuaries (employed by the audit firm), as an auditor's internal expert, to assist in the audit process (including in the role of Reviewing Actuary described later in the section on reporting on regulatory returns), their working papers form part of the audit working papers. Where external actuaries are engaged by the auditor, the actuaries' report and notes of any meetings or discussions with them form part of the audit working papers. (See also ISA (UK and Ireland) 620).

ISA (UK AND IRELAND) 240: THE AUDITOR'S RESPONSIBILITIES RELATING TO FRAUD IN AN AUDIT OF FINANCIAL STATEMENTS

Objectives
The objectives of the auditor are:

(a) To identify and assess the risks of material misstatement of the financial statements due to fraud;

(b) To obtain sufficient appropriate audit evidence regarding the assessed risks of material misstatement due to fraud, through designing and implementing appropriate responses; and

(c) To respond appropriately to fraud or suspected fraud identified during the audit. (paragraph 10)

In accordance with ISA (UK and Ireland) 200, the auditor shall maintain professional skepticism throughout the audit, recognizing the possibility that a material misstatement due to fraud could exist, notwithstanding the auditor's past experience of the honesty and integrity of the entity's management and those charged with governance. (paragraph 12)

When performing risk assessment procedures and related activities to obtain an understanding of the entity and its environment, including the entity's internal control required by ISA (UK and Ireland) 315, the auditor shall perform the procedures in paragraphs 17-24 to obtain information for use in identifying the risks of material misstatement due to fraud. (paragraph 16)

51.   The following are considered to be significant fraud risks which insurers may be subject to:

- Policyholder fraud.

- Fraud by directors and employees.

- Fraud by agents, intermediaries or other related parties.

52.   Responsibility for the prevention and detection of fraud and error lies with those charged with governance of an insurer and of the managing agent of a Lloyd's syndicate, even if they have delegated functions to third parties. In carrying out their responsibilities, the directors have regard to the FSA Principles for Businesses (in particular with regard to the criteria for integrity, skill, care and diligence and management and control) and to requirements issued by the Council of Lloyd's. Equivalent provisions apply to directors of managing agents.

53.   Principle 3 requires a firm to take reasonable care to organise and control its affairs responsibly and effectively with adequate risk management systems. SYSC 3.2.20R(1) requires a firm to make and retain adequate records of matters and dealings (including accounting records) which are the subject of requirements and standards under the regulatory system. Whilst the inherent risk of fraud may continue to exist, the establishment of accounting and internal control systems sufficient to meet these requirements (particularly in the case of insurance companies that accept business involving both a high volume of policies and claims of comparatively low value) frequently reduces the likelihood of fraud giving rise to material misstatements in the financial statements. Guidance on the auditor's consideration of accounting systems and internal controls is provided in ISA (UK and Ireland) 315.

The auditor shall make inquiries of management, and others within the entity as appropriate, to determine whether they have knowledge of any actual, suspected or alleged fraud affecting the entity. (paragraph 18)

In accordance with ISA (UK and Ireland) 315, the auditor shall identify and assess the risks of material misstatement due to fraud at the financial statement level, and at the assertion level for classes of transactions, account balances and disclosures. (paragraph 25)

54.   As with other entities fraud on insurers, either fraudulent financial reporting (for example the manipulation of profits or the concealment of losses) or misappropriation of assets, can occur through a combination of management fraud, employee fraud or fraud perpetrated by third parties. However, fraud risk factors particularly relevant to insurers may be due to the following, for example:

*   The commission driven nature of arrangements with many business introducers whose interests may be more focused on the volume of business and commission thereon rather than the ultimate profitability and sustainability of the business for the insurer. This may increase the risk of fraud committed by agents and intermediaries.

*   The existence of very large estimated liabilities which may not crystallise for many years.

*   Complex insurance and reinsurance transactions provide an opportunity to conceal inappropriate pricing of the risks transferred and to apply inappropriate accounting treatments which may have a significant impact on the results for a given period and the balance sheet position.

*   The transfer of risk under a contract of insurance is not reflected in the passing of any physical asset which can make it difficult for insurers to ensure that all transactions are recorded completely and accurately.

- The nature of delegated underwriting, coupled with large amounts of cash and near liquid assets often held by agents and other intermediaries with delegated authority, increases the propensity for fraud.

- The practice of insurance contracts incepting before all of the terms are agreed and documented provides the opportunity for fraudulent manipulation of contract wordings.

The examples of deficiencies in internal control set out in the section on ISA (UK and Ireland) 315 may be especially relevant when assessing fraud risk.

When identifying and assessing the risks of material misstatement due to fraud, the auditor shall, based on a presumption that there are risks of fraud in revenue recognition, evaluate which types of revenue, revenue transactions or assertions give rise to such risks. (paragraph 26)

55.   In the context of an insurer, "revenue" in respect of insurance contracts may reasonably be taken as earned premiums. However the auditor will also consider the likelihood of fraud in relation to the recognition of income or costs which may have a close relationship to earned premiums, such as reinsurance costs and acquisition costs. Where insurers issue investment contracts that are subject to deposit accounting, "revenue" may reasonably be taken as the fees receivable under those contracts.

56.   Insurers frequently outsource insurance and accounting functions to service companies. Service companies are considered as agents of the insurance companies and the auditor will, therefore, consider the equivalent risk factors for service companies. Further guidance on this issue is contained in the section dealing with ISA (UK and Ireland) 402.

The auditor shall consider whether other information obtained by the auditor indicates risks of material misstatement due to fraud. (paragraph 23)

57.   The auditor considers reports or information obtained from the insurer's compliance department, legal department, and money laundering reporting officer together with reviews undertaken by third parties such as skilled person's reports prepared under section 166 FSMA 2000[15].

---

15   Section 166 FSMA 2000 provides the FSA with the power to require a firm to appoint a skilled person to provide a report on any matter that the FSA may reasonably require in connection with the exercise of the functions conferred on it by or under FSMA 2000. The requirements concerning skilled persons are set out in SUP5.

If the auditor has identified a fraud or has obtained information that indicates that a fraud may exist, the auditor shall communicate these matters on a timely basis to the appropriate level of management in order to inform those with primary responsibility for the prevention and detection of fraud of matters relevant to their responsibilities. (paragraph 40)

The auditor shall include in the audit documentation communications about fraud made to management, those charged with governance, regulators and others. (paragraph 46)

58. Reduction of financial crime is one of the FSA's statutory objectives. The FSA's rules require authorised firms to report "significant" fraud, errors and other irregularities to the FSA (SUP 15.3.17R) (and, where applicable, to the Council of Lloyd's). The auditor is aware of the auditor's duty to report direct to FSA in certain circumstances (see the section of this Practice Note relating to ISA (UK and Ireland) 250 Section B).

Additional considerations relating to Lloyd's
59. Examples of fraud by directors or employees of a managing agent include fraudulent recharges of agency expenses to managed syndicates and fraudulent misallocation of transactions to different years of account within those syndicates. Instances of suspected or actual fraud may involve breaches of specific requirements relating to syndicates and their managing agents as prescribed by Lloyd's in its capacity as market supervisor, and are likely to be regarded as being of material significance. Syndicate auditors have a duty to consider reporting all such instances to the Council of Lloyd's without delay in accordance with their undertaking given to Lloyd's. Guidance on such reporting is contained in the ISA (UK and Ireland) 250 Section B section of this Practice Note.

ISA (UK AND IRELAND) 250: SECTION A – CONSIDERATION OF LAWS AND REGULATIONS IN AN AUDIT OF FINANCIAL STATEMENTS

Objectives

The objectives of the auditor are:

(a) To obtain sufficient appropriate audit evidence regarding compliance with the provisions of those laws and regulations generally recognized to have a direct effect on the determination of material amounts and disclosures in the financial statements;

(b) To perform specified audit procedures to help identify instances of non-compliance with other laws and regulations that may have a material effect on the financial statements; and

(c) To respond appropriately to non-compliance or suspected non-compliance with laws and regulations identified during the audit. (paragraph 10)

As part of obtaining an understanding of the entity and its environment in accordance with ISA (UK and Ireland) 315, the auditor shall obtain a general understanding of:

(a) The legal and regulatory framework applicable to the entity and the industry or sector in which the entity operates; and

(b) How the entity is complying with that framework. (paragraph 12)

The auditor shall obtain sufficient appropriate audit evidence regarding compliance with the provisions of those laws and regulations generally recognized to have a direct effect on the determination of material amounts and disclosures in the financial statements. (paragraph 13)

60. In the context of insurers, laws and regulations are central to the conduct of business if breaches would have either of the following consequences:

   (a) Removal of authorisation to carry out insurance business; or

   (b) The imposition of fines or restrictions on business activities whose significance is such that, where relevant, the ability of the insurer to continue as a going concern is threatened.

61. Non-compliance with laws and regulations that are central to an insurer's activities is likely to give rise to a statutory duty to report to the FSA or a duty to report to the Council of Lloyd's. Such reports are made in accordance with the requirements of ISA (UK and

Ireland) 250 Section B, following the guidance set out in the relevant section of this Practice Note.

62. Insurers are affected by two types of regulation which are central to their activities and of which the auditor needs to obtain a general understanding:

    (a) Prudential supervision; and

    (b) Market conduct rules.

63. The principal purpose of prudential supervision is to ensure the protection of policyholders because of the promissory nature of transactions between insurers and the public. Many of the rules for prudential supervision are based on European Directives. The specific regulatory objectives of the FSA are described in paragraph 28 above.

64. Prudential supervision of insurance companies with their head offices in the UK and insurers established outside the EEA with UK branches is carried out by the FSA under rules made by the FSA under FSMA 2000. Ongoing prudential supervision of authorised insurance companies is conducted in part by means of the annual regulatory returns submitted by all authorised insurance companies and non-EEA insurers with UK branches within three months of their balance sheet date for insurers making electronic submissions (otherwise 2 months and 15 days).

65. Market conduct regulation relates to the sale of business and is primarily carried out by the FSA through its rules in respect of COBS (designated investment business which includes long-term insurance investment business) and ICOBS (general insurance and long-term pure protection business).

Additional considerations relating to Lloyd's

66. For Lloyd's syndicates, prudential supervision of the Lloyd's market as a whole and of managing agents is carried out by the FSA. Additional supervision of syndicates and managing agents is conducted by Lloyd's. Ongoing prudential supervision of the Lloyd's market is carried out by the FSA on a similar basis to insurance companies including the review of an annual regulatory return for the market as a whole submitted within six months of its balance sheet date.

67. There are, in addition, compensation schemes set up to protect individual policyholders for certain classes of business under the Financial Services Compensation Scheme (FSCS) (established under FSMA 2000), and the Motor Insurers' Bureau (established under the Road Traffic Act 1988). Insurers may be required to contribute to levies raised by these guarantee funds depending on the type of insurance business carried on.

68. There are also consumer affairs bodies, such as the Financial Ombudsman Service (which handles consumer complaints) and the Office of Fair Trading (a statutory body which applies to both financial services and other retail organisations).

Additional considerations relating to Lloyd's

69. In the context of Lloyd's syndicates, and their management, the principal laws and regulations are those relevant to insurers as set out above and in addition the requirements prescribed by the Council of Lloyd's, non-compliance with which may reasonably be expected to result in Lloyd's exercising its powers of intervention so as to require the syndicate to cease accepting new business and procure the close of existing business on an orderly basis into a third party.

The auditor shall perform the following audit procedures to help identify instances of non-compliance with other laws and regulations that may have a material effect on the financial statements:

(a) Inquiring of management and, where appropriate, those charged with governance, as to whether the entity is in compliance with such laws and regulations; and

(b) Inspecting correspondence, if any, with the relevant licensing or regulatory authorities. (paragraph 14)

During the audit, the auditor shall remain alert to the possibility that other audit procedures applied may bring instances of non-compliance or suspected non-compliance with laws and regulations to the auditor's attention. (paragraph 15)

70. Specific areas that the auditor's procedures may address include the following:

• Obtaining a general understanding of the legal and regulatory framework applicable to the entity and industry, and of the procedures followed to ensure compliance with the framework.

• The insurer's compliance with prudential capital requirements (including applicable group capital requirements), the results of the insurer's Individual Capital Assessment (ICA), and whether any Individual Capital Guidance has been given by the FSA.

• The insurer's compliance with the scope of its permissions or any limits that may be specified in any Permission Notice issued by the FSA.

- Reviewing correspondence with the FSA and other regulators (including that relating to any FSA supervisory visits, requests for information by FSA or progress concerning FSA ARROW II risk mitigation programmes).

- Holding discussions with the insurer's compliance officer and other personnel responsible for compliance.

- Reviewing compliance reports prepared for the Board, audit committee and other committees.

- Consideration of work on compliance matters performed by internal audit.

- Where an authorised insurer is a parent company, considering the impact of breaches of local laws and regulations on the trading status of the parent company, and of the overseas subsidiary/branch if they are likely to have a material effect on the financial statements of the parent company or group. Regard is also had to the powers of intervention exercisable by the relevant regulatory authorities and the potential impact on the group financial statements.

Additional considerations relating to Lloyd's

71. The process for prudential supervision of the market means that Lloyd's centrally has responsibility for reviewing and agreeing with the managing agent for each syndicate an appropriate amount of prudential capital requirements and for determining how those requirements are to be resourced.

72. In the case of Lloyd's syndicates that undertake business outside the UK, Lloyd's co-ordinates compliance with the requirements of overseas regulatory authorities, and incorporates relevant provisions as necessary in its own regulatory requirements, thus supporting a global operating licence. The auditor of a Lloyd's syndicate that undertakes business overseas therefore does not need to make a separate assessment of the impact of local laws and regulations over and above those specified by Lloyd's.

Money Laundering

Anti-money laundering legislation in the UK and Ireland imposes a duty on the auditor to report suspected money laundering activity. There are similar laws and regulations relating to financing terrorist offences. The detailed legislation in both countries differs but the impact on the auditor can broadly be summarised as follows:

- Partners and staff in audit firms are required to report suspicions of conduct which would constitute a criminal offence which gives rise to direct or indirect benefit.

- Partners and staff in audit firms need to be alert to the dangers of "tipping off" (in the UK) or "prejudicing an investigation" (in Ireland), as this will constitute a criminal offence under the anti-money laundering legislation.

For the UK further detail is set out in Practice Note 12 (Revised): Money Laundering – Guidance for auditors on UK legislation. (paragraph A11-2)

73. Authorised firms including insurers are subject to the requirements of the Money Laundering Regulations 2007 (as amended) and the Proceeds of Crime Act 2002 as well as FSA rules. These laws and regulations require institutions to establish and maintain procedures to identify their customers, establish appropriate reporting and investigation procedures for suspicious transactions, and maintain appropriate records.

74. Laws and regulations relating to money laundering are integral to the legal and regulatory framework within which insurers conduct their business. By the nature of their business, insurers are ready targets of those engaged in money laundering activities. The effect of this legislation is to make it an offence to provide assistance to those involved in money laundering and makes it an offence not to report suspicions of money laundering to the appropriate authorities, usually the Serious Organised Crime Agency ("SOCA"). FSA requirements are set out in SYSC 3.2.6AR – 3.2.6JG. In this context, the FSA has due regard to compliance with the relevant provisions of guidance issued by the Joint Money Laundering Steering Group ("JMLSG")(SYSC 3.2.6EG).

75. In addition to considering whether an insurer has complied with the money laundering laws and regulations, the auditor has reporting obligations under the Proceeds of Crime Act, 2002 and the Money Laundering Regulations, 2007 (as amended) to report knowledge or suspicion of money laundering offences, including those arising from fraud and theft, to SOCA. The auditor is aware of the prohibition on "tipping off" when discussing money laundering matters with the insurer. Given the nature of insurance business and the likely frequency of needing to report to SOCA the auditor is aware of the short-form[16] of reporting to SOCA that can be used in appropriate circumstances to report minor and usually numerous items.

76. The auditor, in the context of money laundering, is aware of the auditor's duty to report direct to FSA in certain circumstances (see the section of this Practice Note relating to ISA (UK and Ireland) 250 Section B).

---

16 These are termed limited intelligence value reports.

ISA (UK AND IRELAND) 250: SECTION B – THE AUDITOR'S RIGHT AND DUTY TO REPORT TO REGULATORS IN THE FINANCIAL SECTOR

Objective
The objective of the auditor of a regulated entity is to bring information of which the auditor has become aware in the ordinary course of performing work undertaken to fulfil the auditor's audit responsibilities to the attention of the appropriate regulator as soon as practicable when:

(a) The auditor concludes that it is relevant to the regulator's functions having regard to such matters as may be specified in statute or any related regulations; and

(b) In the auditor's opinion there is reasonable cause to believe it is or may be of material significance to the regulator. (paragraph 8)

Where an apparent breach of statutory or regulatory requirements comes to the auditor's attention, the auditor shall:

(a) Obtain such evidence as is available to assess its implications for the auditor's reporting responsibilities;

(b) Determine whether, in the auditor's opinion, there is reasonable cause to believe that the breach is of material significance to the regulator; and

(c) Consider whether the apparent breach is criminal conduct that gives rise to criminal property and, as such, should be reported to the specified authorities. (paragraph 12)

Auditor's duty to report to the FSA
77.   Under the 2001 Regulations, the auditor has duties in certain circumstances to make reports to the FSA. The 2001 Regulations do not require the auditor to perform any additional audit work as a result of the statutory duty nor is the auditor required specifically to seek out breaches of the requirements applicable to a particular authorised person. Information and opinions to be communicated are those meeting the criteria set out below which relate to matters of which the auditor[17] of the authorised person (also referred to below as a "regulated entity") has become aware:

(a) In its capacity as auditor of the authorised person; and

---

17 An "auditor" is defined for this purpose in the 2001 Regulations as a person who is, or has been, an auditor of an authorised person appointed under, or as a result of, a statutory provision including section 340 FSMA 2000.

(b) If it is also the auditor of a person who has close links with the authorised person, in its capacity as auditor of that person.

78. The criteria for determining the matters to be reported are as follows:

(a) The auditor reasonably believes that there is, or has been, or may be, or may have been a contravention of any "relevant requirement" that applies to the person[18] concerned and that contravention may be of material significance to the FSA in determining whether to exercise, in relation to that person, any of its functions under FSMA 2000; or

(b) The auditor reasonably believes that the information on, or its opinion on, those matters may be of material significance to the FSA in determining whether the person concerned satisfies and will continue to satisfy the "Threshold Conditions"[19]; or

(c) The auditor reasonably believes that the person concerned is not, may not be, or may cease to be, a going concern; or

(d) The auditor is precluded from stating in its report that the annual accounts have been properly prepared in accordance with CA 2006 or, where applicable, give a true and fair view or have been prepared in accordance with relevant rules and legislation.

79. In relation to 78(a) above, "relevant requirement" is a requirement by or under FSMA 2000 which relates to authorisation under FSMA 2000 or to the carrying on of any regulated activity. This includes not only relevant statutory instruments but also the FSA's rules (other than the Listing Rules) including the Principles for Businesses. The duty to report also covers any requirement imposed by or under any other Act[20] the contravention of which constitutes an offence which the FSA has the power to prosecute under FSMA 2000. In relation to 78(b) above the duty to report relates to either information or opinions held by the auditor which may be of significance to the FSA in determining whether the regulated entity satisfies and will continue to satisfy the Threshold Conditions. The duty to report opinions, as well as information, allows for circumstances where adequate information on a matter may not readily be forthcoming from the regulated entity, and where judgments need to be made.

---

18 In this context the person is an "Authorised Person".

19 The Threshold Conditions are set out in Schedule 6 to FSMA 2000 and represent the minimum conditions that a firm is required to satisfy and continue to satisfy to be given and to retain Part IV permission. The FSA's guidance on compliance with the Threshold Conditions is contained in the COND module of the FSA Handbook.

20 Examples include the Proceeds of Crime Act 2002 and prescribed regulations relating to money laundering.

**THE AUDITING
PRACTICES BOARD**

Material significance

80. Determining whether a contravention of a relevant requirement or a Threshold Condition is reportable under the 2001 Regulations involves consideration both of whether the auditor "reasonably believes" and that the matter in question "is, or is likely to be, of material significance" to the regulator.

81. The 2001 Regulations do not require the auditor to perform any additional audit work as a result of the statutory duty nor is the auditor required specifically to seek out breaches of the requirements applicable to a particular regulated entity. However, in circumstances where the auditor identifies that a reportable matter may exist, it carries out such extra work, as it considers necessary, to determine whether the facts and circumstances cause the auditor "reasonably to believe" that the matter does in fact exist. It should be noted that the auditor's work does not need to prove that the reportable matter exists.

82. ISA (UK and Ireland) 250 Section B requires that, where an apparent breach of statutory or regulatory requirements comes to the auditor's attention, it obtains such evidence as is available to assess its implications for the auditor's reporting responsibilities and determines whether, in its opinion, there is reasonable cause to believe that the breach is of material significance to the regulator.

Material Significance: the term "material significance" requires interpretation in the context of the specific legislation applicable to the regulated entity. A matter or group of matters is normally of material significance to a regulator's functions when, due either to its nature or its potential financial impact, it is likely of itself to require investigation by the regulator...' (paragraph 9(d))

83. "Material significance" does not have the same meaning as materiality in the context of the audit of financial statements. Whilst a particular event may be trivial in terms of its possible effect on the financial statements of an entity, it may be of a nature or type that is likely to change the perception of the regulator. The determination of whether a matter is, or is likely to be, of material significance to the FSA inevitably requires the auditor to exercise its judgment. In forming such judgments, the auditor needs to consider not simply the facts of the matter but also their implications. In addition, it is possible that a matter, which is not materially significant in isolation, may become so when other possible breaches are considered.

84. The auditor of a regulated entity bases its judgment of "material significance" to the FSA solely on its understanding of the facts of which it is aware without making any assumptions about the information available to the FSA in connection with any particular regulated entity.

85.   Minor breaches of the FSA's rules that, for example, are unlikely to jeopardise the entity's assets or amount to misconduct or mismanagement would not normally be of "material significance". ISA (UK and Ireland) 250 Section B however requires the auditor of regulated entities, when reporting on their financial statements, to review information obtained in the course of the audit and to assess whether the cumulative effect is of "material significance" such as to give rise to a duty to report to the regulator. In circumstances where the auditor is uncertain whether it may be required to make a report or not, it may wish to consider taking legal advice.

86.   On completion of its investigations, the auditor ensures that the facts and circumstances, and the basis for its conclusion as to whether these are, or are likely to be of "material significance" to the FSA, are adequately documented such that the reasons for its decision to report or not, as the case may be, may be clearly demonstrated.

87.   Whilst confidentiality is an implied term of an auditor's contract with a regulated entity, section 342 FSMA 2000 states that an auditor does not contravene that duty if it reports to the FSA information or its opinion, if it is acting in good faith and reasonably believes that the information or opinion is relevant to any function of the FSA. The protection afforded is given in respect of information obtained in its capacity as auditor.

Conduct of the audit

The auditor shall ensure that all staff involved in the audit of a regulated entity have an understanding of:

(a) The provisions of applicable legislation;

(b) The regulator's rules and any guidance issued by the regulator; and

(c) Any specific requirements which apply to the particular regulated entity,

appropriate to their role in the audit and sufficient (in the context of that role) to enable them to identify situations they encounter in the course of the audit which may give reasonable cause to believe that a matter should be reported to the regulator. (paragraph 11)

88.   Understanding, commensurate with the individual's role and responsibilities in the audit process, is required of:

(a) The provisions of the 2001 Regulations concerning the auditor's duty to report to the regulator;

(b) The standards and guidance in ISA (UK and Ireland) 250 Section B, and in this section of this Practice Note;

(c) Relevant sections of the FSA Handbook including the Principles for Businesses and the Threshold Conditions; and

(d) In the context of Lloyd's syndicates, the AAB, the relevant requirements established by the Council of Lloyd's.

89.   The auditor includes procedures within its planning process to ensure that members of the audit team have such understanding (in the context of their role) as to enable them to recognise potentially reportable matters, and that such matters are reported to the audit engagement partner without delay so that a decision may be made as to whether a duty to report arises.

90.   An audit firm appointed as auditor of a regulated entity needs to have in place appropriate procedures to ensure that the audit engagement partner is made aware of any other relationship which exists between any department of the firm and the regulated entity when that relationship could affect the firm's work as auditor (this matter is covered in more detail in Appendix 2 of ISA (UK and Ireland) 250 Section B). The auditor also requests the regulated entity to advise it when the entity appoints a third party (including another department or office of the same firm) to review, investigate or report on any aspects of its business activities that may be relevant to the audit of the financial statements and to provide the auditor with copies of reports by such a third party promptly after their receipt. This matter may usefully be referred to in the engagement letter.

Closely linked entities

91.   Where the auditor of a regulated entity is also auditor of a closely linked entity[21], a duty to report arises directly in relation to information relevant to the regulated entity of which the auditor becomes aware in the course of its work as auditor of the closely linked entity.

92.   The auditor establishes during audit planning whether the regulated entity has one or more closely linked entities of which the audit firm is also the auditor. If there are such entities the auditor considers the significance of the closely linked entities and the nature

---

21 An entity has close links with an authorised person for this purpose if the entity is a:
   (a) Parent undertaking of an authorised person;
   (b) Subsidiary undertaking of an authorised person;
   (c) Parent undertaking of a subsidiary undertaking of an authorised person; or
   (d) Subsidiary undertaking of a parent undertaking of an authorised person.

of the issues that might arise which may be of material significance to the regulator of the regulated entity. Such circumstances may involve:

(a) Activities or uncertainties within the closely linked entity which might significantly impair the financial position of the regulated entity;

(b) Money laundering; and, if the closely linked entity is itself regulated,

(c) Matters that the auditor of the closely linked entity is intending to report to its regulator.

93. Following the risk assessment referred to in the preceding paragraph, the auditor of the regulated entity identifies the closely related entities for which the procedures in this paragraph are necessary. The engagement team of the regulated entity communicates to the engagement team of the selected closely linked entities the audit firm's responsibilities to report to the FSA under the 2001 Regulations and notifies the engagement team of the circumstances that have been identified which, if they exist, might be of material significance to the FSA as regulator of the regulated entity. Prior to completion the auditor of the regulated entity obtains details from the auditor of the closely linked entity of such circumstances or confirmation, usually in writing, that such circumstances do not exist. Where the closely linked entities are part of the inter-auditor group reporting process these steps can be built into that process.

94. Whilst confidentiality is an implied term of an auditor's contract with a regulated entity, section 343 FSMA 2000 states that an auditor of an entity closely linked to an authorised person who is also the auditor of that authorised person does not contravene that duty if it reports to the FSA information or its opinion, if the auditor is acting in good faith and reasonably believes that the information or opinion is relevant to any function of the FSA. The protection afforded is given in respect of information obtained in the capacity of auditor.

95. No duty to report is imposed on the auditor of an entity closely linked to a regulated entity who is not also auditor of the regulated entity.

96. In circumstances where it is not also the auditor of the closely linked entity, the auditor of the regulated entity decides whether there are any matters to be reported to the FSA relating to the affairs of the regulated entity in the light of the information that it receives about a closely linked entity for the purpose of auditing the financial statements of the regulated entity. If the auditor becomes aware of possible matters that may fall to be reported, it may wish to obtain further information from the management or auditor of the closely linked entity to ascertain whether the matter should be reported. To facilitate such possible discussions, at the planning stage of the audit, the auditor of the regulated entity will have considered whether arrangements need to be put in place to allow the auditor to communicate with the management and auditor of the closely linked entity. If the auditor of the regulated entity is unable to communicate with the management and

auditor of the closely linked entity to obtain further information concerning the matters it has identified the auditor of the regulated entity reports the matters, and that it has been unable to obtain further information, direct to the FSA.

Information received in a capacity other than as auditor

97.   There may be circumstances where it is not clear whether information about a regulated entity coming to the attention of the auditor is received in the capacity of auditor or in some other capacity, for example as a general adviser to the entity. Appendix 2 to ISA (UK and Ireland) 250 Section B provides guidance as to how information obtained in non-audit work may be relevant to the auditor in the planning and conduct of the audit and the steps that need to be taken to ensure the communication of information that is relevant to the audit.

Discussing matters of material significance with the directors

98.   The directors are the persons principally responsible for the management of the regulated entity. The auditor will, therefore, normally bring a matter of material significance to the attention of the directors, subject to compliance with legislation relating to "tipping off", and seek agreement on the facts and circumstances. However, ISA (UK and Ireland) 250 Section B emphasises that where the auditor concludes that a duty to report arises it should bring the matter to the attention of the regulator without undue delay. The directors may wish to report the matters identified to the FSA themselves and detail the actions taken or to be taken. Whilst such a report from the directors may provide valuable information, it does not relieve the auditor of the statutory duty to report directly to the FSA.

Timing of a report

99.   The duty to report arises once the auditor has concluded that it reasonably believes that the matter is or is likely to be of material significance to the FSA's regulatory function. In reaching its conclusion the auditor may wish to take appropriate legal or other advice and consult with colleagues.

100.   The report should be made without undue delay once a conclusion has been reached. Unless the matter casts doubt on the integrity of the directors this should not preclude discussion of the matter with the directors and seeking such further advice as is necessary, so that a decision can be made on whether or not a duty to report exists. Such consultations and discussions are, however, undertaken on a timely basis to enable the auditor to conclude on the matter without undue delay.

Auditor's right to report to the FSA

101.   Section 342 FSMA 2000 provides that no duty to which an auditor of an authorised person is subject shall be contravened by communicating in good faith to the FSA information or an opinion on a matter that the auditor reasonably believes is relevant to any functions of the FSA. For this purpose, "authorised person" is deemed to include a Lloyd's syndicate.

102. The scope of the duty to report is wide particularly since, under the FSA's Principle for Businesses 11, an authorised firm must disclose to the FSA appropriately anything relating to the authorised firm of which the FSA would reasonably expect notice. However, in circumstances where the auditor concludes that a matter does not give rise to a statutory duty to report but nevertheless should be brought to the attention of the regulator, in the first instance it advises the directors of its opinion. Where the auditor is unable to obtain, within a reasonable period, adequate evidence that the directors have properly informed the FSA of the matter, then the auditor makes a report to the regulator without undue delay.

103. The auditor may wish to take legal advice before deciding whether, and in what form, to exercise its right to make a report direct to the regulator in order to ensure, for example, that only relevant information is disclosed and that the form and content of its report is such as to secure the protection of FSMA 2000. However, the auditor recognises that legal advice will take time and that speed of reporting is likely to be important in order to protect the interests of customers and/or to enable the FSA to meet its statutory objectives.

Additional considerations relating to Lloyd's

Lloyd's syndicates

104. The auditor of a syndicate needs to consider whether it is under a duty or right to report on a particular matter to the FSA, to the Council of Lloyd's or to both.

105. The duty to report matters of material significance applies to all engagements carried out by recognised accountants. Recognised accountants are not required to carry out procedures to detect matters of material significance. This applies even when the recognised accountant is reporting on specific issues under paragraph 13 of the AAB such that the focus of the work undertaken is very narrow.

106. The key factor in determining when a duty arises is the existence of circumstances that would either lead to suspension of authorisation to operate in the Lloyd's market or that warrant use of Lloyd's power of intervention in an individual entity's conduct of business.

107. Under paragraph 6(6) of the AAB, any appointment of a recognised accountant shall include the consent and waiver provisions set out in Schedule 3 to the AAB. These require the syndicate's managing agent to acknowledge and declare that no duty which the recognised accountant might owe to the syndicate or managing agent concerned would be contravened by the recognised accountant communicating in good faith to the Council any information in relation to a matter of which it has become aware in the ordinary course of work undertaken to fulfil its responsibilities

as syndicate auditor or reporting accountant and which it considers is relevant to any function of the Council under the Lloyd's Act 1982 or any byelaws made thereafter.

108. The undertaking given by the recognised accountant as set out in paragraph 4(3) of Schedule 2 of the AAB provides that the recognised accountant undertakes to report to the Council of Lloyd's without delay information of which it becomes aware in the ordinary course of performing either work undertaken to fulfil its audit responsibilities or work undertaken to fulfil its responsibilities as reporting accountant for a syndicate when in its opinion there is reasonable cause to believe that:

    (a) The authorisation of the syndicate or managing agent could be withdrawn; or

    (b) There is or may be a failure to fulfil relevant criteria of sound and prudent management which is or may be of material significance to Lloyd's in determining whether any of its powers of intervention should be exercised; or

    (c) There is or may be breach of the provisions of the Lloyd's Acts 1871 to 1982 (or related byelaws or regulations) which is likely to be of material significance to Lloyd's, such that its powers of intervention should be exercised; or

    (d) The continuous functioning of the syndicate or managing agent may be affected; or

    (e) The recognised accountant concludes that it cannot issue its report without qualifying its opinion.

109. In accordance with the undertaking given in the form set out in Schedule 2 to the AAB, the recognised accountant agrees to the extent that it may do so lawfully and ethically, to provide the Council with such information, documents and explanations in relation to matters which it has a duty to report of which it has become aware.

110. Taken together, the consent and waiver given by the managing agent of the syndicate and the undertaking given by the recognised accountant provide that a recognised accountant is able to communicate to the Council on any matters which, in the opinion of the recognised accountant, is or may be relevant to any function of Lloyd's as regulator relating to the entity's affairs arising out of the work carried out to fulfil responsibilities as syndicate auditor or reporting accountant. However, the recognised accountant is not protected from any breach of duty if, in making a report to the Council, the reporting accountant does not act in good faith. Accordingly, recognised accountants may wish to take appropriate legal or other professional advice before taking the decision whether, and if so, in what manner, to report to the Council.

111. Furthermore, the recognised accountant undertakes to report information of which it becomes aware in the ordinary course of performing the work carried out to fulfil

responsibilities as syndicate auditor or reporting accountant which relates to any other entity regulated by the Council. This extends to any other entity having close links arising from a control relationship with the entity in relation to which the recognised accountant is performing that work.

112. If the recognised accountant, after becoming aware of a matter giving rise to a statutory duty to report, fails to report either without delay or at all, the Council can take action under paragraph 5(3) of the AAB to remove them from the list of recognised accountants. Action could also be taken by the recognised accountants' own regulatory body.

113. The Council accords particular importance to timely notification of matters giving rise to such a report to the Council by recognised accountants. ISA (UK and Ireland) 250 Section B acknowledges that recognised accountants will normally seek evidence to assess the implications of a suspected breach before reporting a matter. Once they have identified information as being subject to the duty to report, ISA (UK and Ireland) 250 Section B requires them to bring it to the attention of the regulator without delay. A recognised accountant may fail to discharge its duty to report to the Council if it waits until giving its formal opinion on the financial statements of a syndicate, or (in its capacity as reporting accountant on syndicates appointed under paragraph 13 of the AAB) on other ad hoc reports, or if they agree to delay making a report until management has had the opportunity to take remedial action.

114. The auditor of a Lloyd's syndicate is required under paragraph 9 of the AAB to give notice to Lloyd's of its resignation, removal or retirement and under paragraph 10 of the AAB such notice shall be accompanied by a statement signed by the auditor to the effect that there are no circumstances connected with its ceasing to hold office which it considers should be brought to the attention of the members of the syndicate or to the managing agent or by a statement by the auditor specifying all such circumstances. In addition the auditor of a Lloyd's syndicate is required to notify the FSA of its resignation, removal or retirement as set out above.

Lloyd's corporate members
115. Auditors of Lloyd's corporate members are required by the Lloyd's Membership Byelaw to give an undertaking to Lloyd's that includes the following clause:

"The auditor undertakes to use its best endeavours, to the extent that it may do so lawfully and ethically, having regard to any relevant guidance on confidentiality to provide to the Council such information or opinions in relation to matters of which it has become aware in its capacity as auditor of the Lloyd's corporate member for the purpose of the exercise by the Council of powers contained in Lloyd's Acts 1871 to 1982 or in byelaws or regulations made thereunder whether or not in respect to a request by or under the authority of the Council. Therefore, the auditor of a Lloyd's corporate member needs to consider whether it has a duty or right to report a particular matter to Lloyd's."

116. Auditors of Lloyd's corporate members are not required to carry out procedures to detect matters that may be of material significance to Lloyd's.

117. The key factor in determining whether a duty to report to Lloyd's arises is the existence of circumstances that would either lead to suspension of the Lloyd's corporate member's authorisation to operate in the Lloyd's market or warrant use of Lloyd's power of intervention in the Lloyd's corporate member's conduct of business.

118. The undertaking for a Lloyd's corporate member does not specify the matters described above. However, if the auditor concludes that it cannot issue its report without qualifying the opinion then a duty to report would arise. Reference to an emphasis of matter without qualification of the opinion expressed does not of itself give rise to a duty to report to Lloyd's: however, the factors giving rise to an emphasis of matter may themselves do so.

119. The auditor is not protected from any breach of duty if, in making a report to the Council, the auditor does not act in good faith. Accordingly, the auditor may wish to take appropriate legal or other professional advice before taking the decision whether, and if so, in what manner, to report to the Council.

120. The duty to report to Lloyd's for auditors of Lloyd's corporate members does not extend to any other entity that has close links with the Lloyd's corporate member.

121. The Council accords particular importance to timely notification of matters giving rise to such a report to the Council by auditors of Lloyd's corporate members. ISA (UK and Ireland) 250 Section B acknowledges that the auditor will normally seek evidence to assess the implications of a suspected breach before reporting a matter. Once it has identified information as being subject to the duty to report, ISA (UK and Ireland) 250 Section B requires it to bring the matter to the attention of the regulator without delay. An auditor may fail to discharge its duty to report to the Council if it waits until giving its formal opinion on the financial statements of the corporate member or on other ad hoc reports, or if it agrees to delay making a report until management has had the opportunity to take remedial action.

ISA (UK AND IRELAND) 300: PLANNING AN AUDIT OF FINANCIAL STATEMENTS

Objective
The objective of the auditor is to plan the audit so that it will be performed in an effective manner. (paragraph 4)

The auditor shall establish an overall audit strategy that sets the scope, timing and direction of the audit, and that guides the development of the audit plan. (paragraph 7)

The auditor shall develop an audit plan that shall include a description of:

(a) The nature, timing and extent of planned risk assessment procedures, as determined under ISA (UK and Ireland) 315.

(b) The nature, timing and extent of planned further audit procedures at the assertion level, as determined under ISA (UK and Ireland) 330.

(c) Other planned audit procedures that are required to be carried out so that the engagement complies with ISAs (UK and Ireland) (paragraph 9)

122. In planning the audit of an insurer, the auditor obtains a detailed understanding of the particular types of insurance business undertaken. The planning process includes discussion with the insurer's management and, in particular may include those with responsibility for:

- Determining, implementing and monitoring underwriting policy.
- Technical provisions.
- Managing investments.
- Compliance and regulation.

123. Matters the auditor of an insurer may consider as part of the planning process for the audit of the financial statements include:

- The nature and scope of the insurer's business.
- The insurer's relationships with the FSA and any other regulators.
- Changes in applicable laws, regulations and accounting requirements.
- Issues relating to the auditor's statutory duty to report.

Guidance on the first three matters is included in the section on ISA (UK and Ireland) 315 and on the fourth matter in the section on ISA (UK and Ireland) 250 Section B.

124. In addition, particular issues likely to require consideration in planning the audit are:

(a) The need to involve auditor's experts. The nature and complexity of insurance businesses increase the likelihood that the auditor may consider it necessary, in order to obtain sufficient appropriate evidence on which to base its report, to involve auditor's experts in the audit process. For example, the auditor may wish to rely on the work of an actuary or a statistician to assist its consideration of an insurer's technical provisions. Other auditor's experts the auditor may consider involving include regulatory, investment and systems specialists. Consequently, the auditor of an insurer considers the need to involve such auditor's experts at an early stage in planning its work. Where such auditor's experts are to be used, they may take part in discussions with the insurer's management and staff, in order to assist in the development of knowledge and understanding relating to the insurer's business. As part of the planning process the auditor agrees in advance the scope of work of the auditor's actuarial and other experts, including the scope of their reports;

(b) The need to include in the engagement team persons using expertise in a specialized area of accounting or auditing, whether engaged or employed by the auditing firm who performs audit procedures on the engagement. The application of relevant tax legislation is likely to be complex, and hence the auditor may wish to involve a tax specialist to assist the consideration of provisions for corporation and other taxes included in an insurer's financial statements; and

(c) The effect of delegated authorities granted by the insurer, and the sources of evidence available to the auditor for transactions undertaken by those to whom such authority has been given. The auditor of an insurer considers the implications of delegated authorities in planning its work. This may include the outsourcing of certain functions, such as investment management or the delegation of authority to underwrite and/or administer business, and to process and/or settle claims.

125. In the case of an insurer reporting under UK GAAP undertaking long-term insurance business (other than a Lloyd's corporate member), its Reporting Actuary plays a central role in advising the insurer's board on the determination of the long-term business technical provision disclosed in its financial statements. The auditor discusses elements of its audit plan with the Reporting Actuary, in order to ensure that its audit procedures have regard to the Reporting Actuary's work. Where the insurer appoints a separate actuary to fulfil the duties of the actuarial function holder or the with-profits actuary in relation to the insurer's regulatory obligations, the auditor also considers the need for liaison with these individuals.

126. The scope of the work to be performed by the Reviewing Actuary in respect of both the statutory audit and the audit of the regulatory return is agreed and documented during

the planning stages of the audit. Consequently, it is advantageous for the Reviewing Actuary to participate in the planning process.

127. In view of its responsibility to report on regulatory returns, the auditor of an authorised insurer plans its work so as to carry out procedures necessary both to form an opinion on the financial statements and to report on matters included in the regulatory returns in an efficient and effective manner.

Additional considerations relating to Lloyd's

128. A syndicate auditor plans its work so as to carry out procedures necessary both to form an opinion on the financial statements and to report separately as to whether the procedures and controls provide assurance that:

   (a) Underwriting members' personal accounts and syndicate MAPA accounts have been prepared in accordance with the Syndicate Accounting Byelaw; and

   (b) Net results shown in underwriting members' personal accounts and syndicate MAPA accounts have been calculated in accordance with the applicable agency agreements.

129. Much of the business conducted in the Lloyd's market uses central services in areas such as policy preparation, claims adjustment and transaction settlement. The service provider's Independent Service Auditor's Report on the operation of systems of control relates to certain of the relevant accounting information systems. As part of audit planning a syndicate auditor considers the extent to which it intends to place reliance on such reports.

ISA (UK AND IRELAND) 315: IDENTIFYING AND ASSESSING THE RISKS OF MATERIAL MISSTATEMENT THROUGH UNDERSTANDING THE ENTITY AND ITS ENVIRONMENT

Objective

The objective of the auditor is to identify and assess the risks of material misstatement, whether due to fraud or error, at the financial statement and assertion levels, through understanding the entity and its environment, including the entity's internal control, thereby providing a basis for designing and implementing responses to the assessed risks of material misstatement. (paragraph 3)

130. Insurers can be complex and the auditor seeks to understand the business and the regulatory regime in which they operate. Generally, there is a close relationship between planning and obtaining an understanding of the entity and its environment, which is covered more fully below.

The auditor shall obtain an understanding of the following:

(a) Relevant industry, regulatory, and other external factors including the applicable financial reporting framework.

(b) The nature of the entity, including:

(i) its operations;

(ii) its ownership and governance structures;

(iii) the types of investments that the entity is making and plans to make, including investments in special purpose entities; and

(iv) the way that the entity is structured and how it is financed to enable the auditor to understand the classes of transactions, account balances, and disclosures to be expected in the financial statements. (paragraph 11(a) and (b))

131. When obtaining an understanding of the insurer's business, the auditor considers, for example:

- The methods by which business is transacted including whether the insurer participates with others in contracts for large commercial risks, and if so whether it transacts business as "leader" in such contracts or as a "follower".

- The characteristics of its insurance products, including those written in previous years where exposure remains.

- The introduction of new categories of products or customers or distribution channels.

- The reinsurance arrangements.

- The complexity of the insurer's information systems.

- The legal and operational structure of the insurer.

- The number and location of branches.

- The regulatory capital position.

- Changes in the market environment (for example, a marked increase in competition).

- Relevant economic developments.

- Developments in relevant legislation and changes resulting from new judicial decisions.

132. Insurance policies written in previous years may continue to have an impact upon insurers' financial statements in subsequent years. For example, for general insurance business the terms of the insurance cover provided and the reinsurance arrangements in force in a previous year are factors involved in the determination of technical provisions not only in the year in which the claims are incurred, but also in subsequent periods if the original estimates of the claims in question change. Similarly for life assurance business guarantees and options and other policyholder promises made on the issue of policies in prior years will be one of the key factors in determining estimates for related technical provisions.

133. In obtaining an understanding of the regulatory factors the auditor considers, for example:

- Any formal communications between the FSA in its capacity as the regulator and the insurer, including any new or interim risk assessments issued by the FSA and the results of any other supervisory visits conducted by the FSA.

- The contents of any recent reports prepared by "skilled persons" under section 166 of FSMA 2000 together with any correspondence, minutes or notes of meetings relevant to any recent skilled persons' report.

- Any formal communications between the insurer and other regulators.

- Discussions with the insurer's compliance officer together with others responsible for monitoring regulatory compliance.

The auditor shall obtain an understanding of the entity's selection and application of accounting policies, including the reasons for changes thereto. The auditor shall evaluate whether the entity's accounting policies are appropriate for its business and consistent with the applicable financial reporting framework and accounting policies used in the relevant industry. (paragraph 11(c))

134. Accounting policies of particular relevance may include those in relation to insurance and investment contracts, embedded derivatives in insurance contracts, deferred acquisition costs, classification of assets and liabilities (and thereby their measurement) and revenue recognition (including investment management service contracts). The auditor undertakes procedures to consider whether the policies adopted are in compliance with applicable accounting standards and gains an understanding of the procedures, systems and controls applied to maintain compliance with them.

The auditor shall obtain an understanding of the entity's objectives and strategies, and those related business risks that may result in material misstatement. (paragraph 11(d))

135. It is important for the auditor to understand the multi-dimensional nature and extent of the financial and business risks which are integral to the environment, and how the insurer's systems record and address these risks. Although they may apply to varying degrees, the risks include (but are not limited to):

- Underwriting or insurance risk: which is inherent in any insurance business but will be influenced by, for example, the classes of business underwritten, new products or services introduced and guarantees given.

- Credit risk: at its simplest, this is the risk that a third party will be unable to meet its obligations (for example, recoveries from reinsurers).

- Liquidity risk: the risk that arises from the possibility that an insurer has insufficient liquid funds to meet claims.

- Interest rate risk: the risk that arises where there is a mismatch between the interest rate reset dates or bases used for asset and liability measurement.

- Currency risk: the risk that arises from the mismatching of assets, liabilities and commitments denominated in different currencies.

- Market risk: the risk that changes in the value of assets, liabilities and commitments will occur as a result of movements in relative prices (for example, as a result of changes in the market price of tradable assets).

- Pension obligation risk: the risk that the insurer's obligations towards its pension schemes may lead to the insurer not being able to pay its other liabilities as they fall due; and the risk that an increase in the funding requirements results in a significant reduction in the insurer's capital resources.

- Operational risk: the risk of loss, arising from inadequate or failed internal processes, people or systems or from external events, including legal risk.

- Regulatory risk: the risk of public censure, fines (together with related compensation payments) and restriction or withdrawal of authorisation to conduct some or all of the insurer's activities. In the UK this may arise from enforcement activity by the FSA.

Failure to manage the risks outlined above can also cause serious damage to an insurer's reputation, potentially leading to loss of confidence in the insurer's business (this is sometimes referred to as reputational risk).

> The auditor shall obtain an understanding of the measurement and review of the entity's financial performance (paragraph 11(e)).

136. The auditor obtains an understanding of the measures used by management to review the insurer's performance. Further guidance on key performance indicators is given in the section on ISA (UK and Ireland) 520.

> The auditor shall obtain an understanding of internal control relevant to the audit. Although most controls relevant to the audit are likely to relate to financial reporting, not all controls that relate to financial reporting are relevant to the audit. It is a matter of the auditor's professional judgment whether a control, individually or in combination with others, is relevant to the audit. (paragraph 12)
>
> When obtaining an understanding of controls that are relevant to the audit, the auditor shall evaluate the design of those controls and determine whether they have been implemented, by performing procedures in addition to inquiry of the entity's personnel. (paragraph 13)
>
> The auditor shall obtain an understanding of the control environment. As part of obtaining this understanding, the auditor shall evaluate whether:
>
> (a) Management, with the oversight of those charged with governance, has created and maintained a culture of honesty and ethical behaviour; and
>
> (b) The strengths in the control environment elements collectively provide an appropriate foundation for the other components of internal control, and whether those other components are not undermined by deficiencies in the control environment. (paragraph 14)

THE AUDITING
PRACTICES BOARD

137. The quality of the overall control environment is dependent upon management's attitude towards the operation of controls. A positive attitude may be evidenced by an organisational framework which enables proper segregation of duties and delegation of control functions and which encourages failings to be reported and corrected. Thus, where a lapse in the operation of a control is treated as a matter of concern, the control environment will be stronger and will contribute to effective control systems; whereas a weak control environment will undermine detailed controls, however well designed. The systems of control need to have regard to the requirements of SYSC and PRIN as well as the provisions of IPRU(INS), INSPRU and GENPRU. Although the directors are required to certify that they are satisfied that throughout the financial year the insurer has complied in all material respects with these requirements, auditors of insurers do not have responsibility for reporting on whether systems of control meet regulatory requirements.

138. The FSA requires authorised firms, including insurers, to maintain systems and controls appropriate for its business[22]. These include (but are not limited to):

- Clear and appropriate reporting lines which are communicated within the insurer.
- Appropriate controls to ensure compliance with laws and regulations (this may mean a separate compliance function).
- Appropriate risk assessment process.
- Appropriate management information.
- Controls to ensure suitability of staff.
- Controls to manage tensions arising out of remuneration policies.
- Documented and tested business continuity plans.
- Documented business plans or strategies.
- An internal audit function (where appropriate).
- An audit committee (where appropriate).
- Appropriate record keeping arrangements.

139. Systems of internal control of an insurer are important in ensuring orderly and prudent operations of the insurer and in assisting the directors to prepare financial statements which give a true and fair view. The following features of the business of insurers may be relevant to the auditor's assessment of such internal controls:

---

22 Most FSA systems and control requirements are set out in SYSC, but additional requirements relating to prudential matters also exist in GENPRU and INSPRU.

- The substantial scale of transactions, both in terms of volume and relative value, makes it important that control systems are in place to ensure that transactions are recorded promptly, accurately and completely and are checked and approved, and that records are reconciled at appropriate intervals in order to identify and investigate differences promptly. Processing and accounting for complex transactions or high volumes of less complex transactions will almost inevitably involve the use of sophisticated technology. For example, transactions subject to "straight through processing" involve little or no manual intervention after they have been initiated.

- Proper segregation of duties between and amongst those writing the risks, those responsible for establishing claims provisions, those responsible for claims handling, those responsible for claims settlement and those recording these transactions, is particularly important.

- Equally as important is the proper segregation of duties between and amongst those responsible for the purchase and sale of investments, those recording these transactions and those responsible for the physical security over the documents of title.

- The geographical or organisational dispersal of some insurers' operations means that, in order to maintain control over its activities, insurers need to ensure not only that there are sufficient controls at each location, but also that there are effective communication and control procedures between the various locations and the centre. It is important that there should be clear, comprehensive reporting and responsibility lines, particularly where the business is managed using a "matrix" structure.

- The activities of insurers can result in the use of complex insurance or reinsurance transactions. The assessment as to whether such transactions transfer risk poses risks of misstatement. Consequently, insurers will normally have developed important operational controls to mitigate such risks of misstatement.

- The provisions of the UK tax legislation are complex for insurers. Accordingly, an effective control system is essential to ensure that the record-keeping requirements of UK tax legislation are satisfied, and that tax is accounted for promptly and accurately. Similar measures may be needed to address similar provisions arising in any other jurisdictions where the insurer operates.

- The UK regulatory framework is both complex and evolving for insurers. This may give rise to significant liabilities for compensation to policyholders if not properly dealt with. Accordingly, an effective control system is essential to ensure that the requirements of the UK regulators are satisfied. Measures may also be needed to address regulators in other jurisdictions.

The auditor shall obtain an understanding of whether the entity has a process for:

(a) Identifying business risks relevant to financial reporting objectives;

(b) Estimating the significance of the risks;

(c) Assessing the likelihood of their occurrence; and

(d) Deciding about actions to address those risks. (paragraph 15)

140. Insurers should undertake appropriate risk assessment procedures as part of their risk management and internal control process under FSA rules. Insurers will normally be required to produce an individual capital assessment (ICA), which is designed to quantify risks specific to the entity and to generate and quantify an estimated capital requirement for the entity. The ICA includes an assessment of operational risk. The auditor will normally review such documentation in assessing the insurer's approach to addressing risks.

The auditor shall obtain an understanding of control activities relevant to the audit, being those the auditor judges it necessary to understand in order to assess the risks of material misstatement at the assertion level and design further audit procedures responsive to assessed risks. An audit does not require an understanding of all the control activities related to each significant class of transactions, account balance, and disclosure in the financial statements or to every assertion relevant to them. (paragraph 20).

141. There is a wide variation between different insurers in terms of size, activity and organisation, so that there can be no standard approach to internal controls and risk. The auditor assesses the adequacy of controls in relation to the circumstances of each entity. Examples of deficiencies in internal control that may be relevant to the auditor's assessment of the risk of material misstatement are as follows:

- Complex products or processes inadequately understood by management; this includes undue concentration of expertise concerning matters requiring the exercise of significant judgment or capable of manipulation such as valuations of financial instruments, insurance or reinsurance contracts.

- Deficiencies in back office procedures undermining the completeness and accuracy of accounting records.

- Deficiencies in new product approval procedures.

- Backlogs in key reconciliations.

- Inadequate maintenance of suspense or clearing accounts.

- Delays in the processing of premiums and claims.

Controls relating to outsourcing activities are considered in the ISA (UK and Ireland) 402 section of this Practice Note.

> In understanding the entity's control activities, the auditor shall obtain an understanding of how the entity has responded to risks arising from IT. (paragraph 21)

142. As a result of the type and complexity of transactions undertaken, and records held, by insurers and the need for swift and accurate information processing and retrieval, many insurers are highly automated, including: the accounting function, the processing of premiums, reinsurance and claims, regulatory reporting and the supply of management information.

143. In addition to providing a basis for preparation of the financial statements and meeting requirements for maintenance of adequate accounting records, a key feature of the information systems maintained by an insurer is the importance of reliable and properly coded historical statistical data to operate the business. Historical statistical data is important, for example, in calculating technical provisions, and for providing analyses for regulatory returns.

144. An effective control system over the administration of insurance business will therefore seek to ensure the accurate collation, processing and storing of large volumes of data relating, for example, to:

- Acceptance of risk.

- Recording of policy details.

- Collection of premiums.

- Recording, investigation, evaluation and payment of claims.

- Identification of classes of business required to be disclosed in the insurer's regulatory returns.

- Transfer of data from the administration systems to systems used for calculating technical provisions.

145. The auditor assesses the extent, nature and impact of automation within the insurer and plans and performs work accordingly. In particular the auditor considers:

   (a) The required level of IT knowledge and skills – these may be extensive and may require the auditor to obtain advice and assistance from staff with specialist skills;

(b) The extent of the application of audit software and related audit techniques;

(c) General controls relating to the environment within which IT based systems are developed, maintained and operated; and

(d) External interfaces susceptible to breaches of security.

146. A single computer system rarely covers all of the insurer's requirements. It is common for insurers to employ a number of different systems and, in many cases, use PC-based applications, sometimes involving the use of complex spreadsheets, to generate important accounting and/or internal control information. The auditor identifies and understands the communication between computer systems in order to assess whether appropriate controls are established and maintained to cover all critical systems and the links between them and to identify the most effective audit approach.

The auditor shall identify and assess the risks of material misstatement at:

(a) The financial statement level.

(b) At the assertion level for classes of transactions, account balances, and disclosures

to provide a basis for designing and performing further audit procedures. (paragraph 25)

As part of the risk assessment as described in paragraph 25, the auditor shall determine whether any of the risks identified are, in the auditor's judgment, a significant risk. In exercising this judgment, the auditor shall exclude the effects of identified controls related to the risk. (paragraph 27)

If the auditor has determined that a significant risk exists, the auditor shall obtain an understanding of the entity's controls, including control activities, relevant to that risk. (paragraph 29)

---

147. Significant risks are likely to arise in those areas that are subject to significant judgment by management or are complex and properly understood by comparatively few people within the insurer.

148. Examples of significant risks for insurers may include:

•   The completeness and accuracy of processing of all insurance transactions (see paragraphs 163-173).

•   The structure of the reinsurance protection programme and the recognition of reinsurance cost and reinsurance recoveries, including the accounting treatment of complex reinsurance arrangements (see paragraphs 174-178).

- Significant measurement uncertainty with respect to technical provisions (see paragraphs 196-212).

149. Deficiencies in the control environment and in controls such as those described in paragraph 141 above could increase the risk of fraud.

150. The application of complex accounting standards such as IAS 32 and 39, IFRS 4 and 7[23], (for insurers using EU-IFRSs) and FRS 25, 26, 27 and 29 (for insurers using UK GAAP) may also give rise to significant risk. This arises from the classification, recognition and measurement of insurance and investment contracts, the classification and measurement of financial assets, hedge accounting, classification of assets/liabilities, revenue/expense recognition. In addition significant risk may arise from the adequacy of financial statement disclosures, notably in respect of insurance and financial risk management.

Additional considerations relating to Lloyd's

151. Responsibility for the establishment and proper operation of systems of control in a Lloyd's syndicate rests with the board of directors of the managing agent.

152. A syndicate auditor is required to report separately on the adequacy of the procedures and controls operated by the managing agent to enable it:

(a) To complete the syndicate's Annual Return; and

(b) To prepare personal accounts

in accordance with the underlying requirements.

153. Responsibility for the establishment and proper operation of systems of control for a Lloyd's corporate member rests with its board of directors. In exercising this responsibility, the directors may conclude that it is appropriate to place reliance on the records maintained, and summaries thereof, prepared by the managing agents of the underlying syndicates and on other, third party documentation. Such records and summaries may, therefore, be considered by the directors to form part of the accounting records of the corporate member. In addition, the directors of the corporate member and its auditor may conclude that it is appropriate to have regard to the work done by other auditors (including syndicate auditors) and to the reports they may issue. Guidance on this matter is set out in the section on ISA (UK and Ireland) 600.

---

23 If the EU adopts IFRS 9 for use in the EU this standard is also likely to give rise to significant risk.

ISA (UK AND IRELAND) 320: MATERIALITY IN PLANNING AND PERFORMING AN AUDIT

Objective
The objective of the auditor is to apply the concept of materiality appropriately in planning and performing the audit. (paragraph 8)

When establishing the overall audit strategy, the auditor shall determine materiality for the financial statements as a whole. If, in the specific circumstances of the entity, there is one or more particular classes of transactions, account balances or disclosures for which misstatement of lesser amounts than materiality for the financial statements as a whole could reasonably be expected to influence the economic decisions of users taken on the basis of the financial statements, the auditor shall also determine the materiality level or levels to be applied to those particular classes of transactions, account balances or disclosures. (paragraph 10)

The auditor shall determine performance materiality for purposes of assessing the risks of material misstatement and determining the nature, timing and extent of further audit procedures. (paragraph 11)

154. The principles of assessing materiality in the audit of an insurer are the same as those applying to the audit of any other entity. In particular the auditor's consideration of materiality is a matter of professional judgment, and is affected by the auditor's perception of the common information needs of users as a group[24].

155. A percentage is often applied to a chosen benchmark as a starting point in determining materiality for the financial statements as a whole. Examples of benchmarks that may be appropriate include categories of reported income, (such as profit before tax, total revenue, and total expenses), total equity or net asset value. Determining a percentage to be applied to the chosen benchmark involves professional judgment based on the circumstances of the insurer. There is a relationship between the percentage and the chosen benchmark such that, for example, a percentage applied to profit before tax will normally be higher than a percentage applied to total revenue. Profit before tax from continuing operations is often used as a benchmark for profit oriented insurers. When profit before tax from continuing operations is volatile, other benchmarks may be more

---

24 The International Accounting Standards Board's "Framework for the Preparation and Presentation of Financial Statements" indicates that, for a profit orientated entity, as investors are providers of risk capital to the enterprise, the provision of financial statements that meets their needs will also meet most of the needs of other users that financial statements can satisfy.

appropriate, such as gross profit or total revenues. Circumstances that give rise to an exceptional increase or decrease in profit before tax from continuing operations may lead the auditor to conclude that materiality for the financial statements as a whole is more appropriately determined using a normalised profit before tax from operations figure, based on past results.

156. However, a key difference of an insurer from other entities is that balance sheet balances tend to be much larger compared to the income statement, so that the application of materiality based on income may be too low when auditing some aspects of elements of the balance sheet.

157. To deal with this, the auditor typically uses materiality based on the income statement if a misstatement in a balance sheet item could affect the income statement or equity and reserves. If, however, a misstatement in a balance sheet item is likely only to lead to a reclassification between line items within assets and liabilities, a higher materiality level can be applied for identifying and evaluating such misstatements only. Although paragraph 10 of ISA (UK and Ireland) 320 indicates that there can only be one overall measure of materiality for the accounts as a whole, paragraph A15 of ISA (UK and Ireland) 450 states that there may be circumstances involving the evaluation of qualitative considerations where the auditor concludes that a classification misstatement is not material in the context of the financial statements as a whole, even though it may exceed the materiality level or levels applied in evaluating other misstatements. For example, a misclassification between balance sheet line items may not be considered material in the context of the financial statements as a whole when the amount of the misclassification is small in relation to the size of the related balance sheet items and the misclassification does not affect the income statement or any key ratios. When applying a separate balance sheet materiality level for the purpose of identifying and evaluating the effect of such misclassifications the auditor considers other relevant factors such as:

• The extent any misstatement of these items would influence the economic decisions of users taken on the basis of the financial statements.

• The extent any misstatement of these items would affect users' expectations regarding the measurement or disclosure of these items.

• The effect of the classification misstatement on debt or other contractual covenants.

• The effect on individual line items or sub-totals.

• The effect on key ratios.

158. Examples of items which may have little or no direct effect on an insurer's income may include:

• Reinsurance arrangements that are entered into to reduce the impact of claims on shareholders' funds. The balance sheet of an insurer is required to include the gross amount of technical provisions within liabilities and any reinsurers' shares of technical provisions within assets. However, a misstatement in the recording of these gross assets and liabilities will have a much lesser effect on the insurer's income statement because the insurer does not bear all of the costs of claims.

- Revenue errors on with-profits business will ordinarily have no impact on income for the year as income is determined by the amount of the bonus distribution.

159. In the case of many classes of insurance business, uncertainty relating to the ultimate cost of claims is an inherent feature of the business. As a result, whilst quantitative measures of materiality are of assistance in directing the focus of the auditor's work, qualitative factors relating to the extent and nature of disclosures in the financial statements will also be of importance. Where such uncertainty is considered to be significant, insurance entity auditors consider the disclosures made in the financial statements, and the effect upon the auditor's report. This matter is dealt with in the sections on ISAs (UK and Ireland) 450, 540 and 705.

ISA (UK AND IRELAND) 330: THE AUDITOR'S RESPONSES TO ASSESSED RISKS

Objective
The objective of the auditor is to obtain sufficient appropriate audit evidence regarding the assessed risks of material misstatement, through designing and implementing appropriate responses to those risks. (paragraph 3)

The auditor shall design and perform tests of control to obtain sufficient appropriate audit evidence as to the operating effectiveness of relevant controls if:

(a) The auditor's assessment of risk of material misstatement at the assertion level includes an expectation that the controls are operating effectively (i.e., the auditor intends to rely on the operating effectiveness of controls in determining the nature, timing and extent of substantive procedures); or

(b) Substantive procedures alone cannot provide sufficient appropriate audit evidence at the assertion level. (paragraph 8)

160. In practice the nature and volume of transactions relating to the operations of insurers often means that performing tests of relevant controls is the most efficient means of reducing audit risk to an acceptably low level.

If the auditor has determined that an assessed risk of material misstatement at the assertion level is a significant risk, the auditor shall perform substantive procedures that are specifically responsive to that risk. When the approach to a significant risk consists only of substantive procedures, those procedures shall include tests of details. (paragraph 21)

161. Examples of significant risks for insurers are set out in paragraph 148.

The auditor shall perform audit procedures to evaluate whether the overall presentation of the financial statements, including the related disclosures, is in accordance with the applicable financial reporting framework. (paragraph 24)

162. Specific accounting standards can require extensive narrative disclosures in the financial statements of insurers; for example, in relation to the nature and extent of risks arising from contracts. In designing and performing procedures to evaluate these disclosures

the auditor obtains audit evidence regarding the assertions about presentation and disclosure described in paragraph A111 of ISA (UK and Ireland) 315 .

Insurance transactions

163. When considering the completeness and accuracy of processing of insurance transactions, the auditor has regard to the multiple purposes for which an insurer will use data entered into its accounting records. Such data may be used not only for inclusion in the financial statements, but may also be included in the regulatory returns of the insurer and be used as the basis for statistical analysis and extrapolation of past trends and transactions in assessing technical provisions. Errors in the data input may therefore have far reaching impact on the overall reported results. Data input required for such other purposes may therefore require additional detail or higher levels of accuracy of coding and allocation compared with those which might be required solely for the preparation of reliable financial statements.

164. For insurance transactions initiated by the insurer, the auditor considers the controls implemented for each material class of business and location, together with overall controls applied by the accounting function and management. Matters for consideration will include the procedures for the setting of and monitoring of compliance with guidelines for underwriting and product development, and controls over completeness of transactions and risks undertaken. Insurers often transact very large volumes of transactions which are subject to extensive IT controls, so the use of computer-assisted audit techniques may be appropriate.

165. The auditor of an insurer also has regard to the procedures implemented by the insurer to ensure the completeness, accuracy and reliability of information provided by third parties, including intermediaries and agents. The auditor assesses the effectiveness of management's controls implemented to ensure that all risks bound by agents under delegated authorities have been included. Procedures include reviewing the insurer's procedures for the approval of such arrangements and the monitoring of the performance of business introduced through such contracts. These may include inspections by the insurer or third parties of the agent's underwriting activities, records and reports to the insurer.

166. The auditor reviews the contractual terms, and assess the extent to which such agents are reporting transactions on a regular and prompt basis and whether the insurer has completely and accurately recorded the reported transactions in the accounting records and statistical databases. Specific consideration will be paid to the terms of the agent's remuneration to ensure for example that all profit commission and expenses recovery entitlements have been recognised.

167. Where significant insurance risks are underwritten through treaty reinsurance contracts, the nature and complexity of the risks written may differ substantially from those written by the insurer directly. The auditor ascertains the insurer's procedures for approving

such contracts, whether relevant transactions are reported regularly and promptly (commonly monthly or quarterly), and whether the insurer has included all such transactions in the accounting records.

168. Reinsurers maintain records of all treaties and may receive regular statements from the cedant of premiums received, claims paid and other data relating to the treaty. The reinsurer may be reliant upon the cedant's statements to maintain accounting records of the underlying treaty transactions.

169. Although a reinsurer may have contractual rights to inspect a cedant's books, it is not uncommon for directors to construct the financial records of the reinsurer from cedant statements. The auditor may obtain evidence that controls in relation to treaty reinsurance exist to ensure that:

    (a) Statements from the ceding insurer are received and processed on a regular basis;

    (b) Statements are reconciled to the reinsurer's accounting records where appropriate; and

    (c) A procedure exists for the regular review of major treaty results.

170. An important aspect of an insurer's controls over completeness and accuracy of processing will often be its procedures for the reconciliation of balances with third parties, the settlement of transactions (including their correction where necessary) and the agreement and clearance of old items. Third parties will include policyholders, brokers, underwriting agents and reinsurers, and procedures may vary for each category. The auditor reviews the insurer's processes and monitoring procedures established to ascertain whether such reconciliations and settlements are up to date. The auditor pays particular attention to the use of suspense or similar accounts, and to whether they are reconciled and cleared regularly and promptly.

171. A significant issue in the audit of insurers is the assessment of whether or not contracts to which the insurers are party should be accounted for as contracts of insurance (or reinsurance). In forming this assessment accounting conventions may require consideration of the level of insurance risk transferred, although the definition of insurance risk and the level of insurance risk required for a contract to be accounted for as insurance (or reinsurance) may vary dependent on whether the insurer is preparing financial statements in accordance with International Financial Reporting Standards or United Kingdom financial reporting standards and on the financial reporting standards in force from time to time.

172. The auditor obtains sufficient, appropriate audit evidence that insurers have properly assessed the level of insurance risk for the purpose of determining whether material contracts or groups of contracts should be accounted for as insurance (or reinsurance), taking into account the applicable accounting requirements.

173. In evaluating the insurer's mechanism for assessing the level of insurance risk, the auditor may consider the following:

- The process adopted by the insurer.

- The likelihood of loss falling to both insurer and reinsurer under different loss scenarios and the probability of occurrence of the scenarios selected for this exercise.

- The cash flow implications under different loss scenarios.

- Any penalty, default or adjustable clauses in the contract.

- The existence and operation of any experience account.

- The existence and operation of other arrangements, whether or not described as reinsurance, that have the effect of limiting the risk transferred by the reinsurance arrangement under review, either by amending the arrangement (e.g. by means of a "side letter") or by counteracting it (e.g. by re-assumption of the same risk by a separate contract).

Reinsurance

174. When considering the impact of the insurer's reinsurance arrangements on the financial statements the auditor obtains an understanding of the reinsurance programme, including both facultative and treaty arrangements. The auditor assesses the procedures for the approval of reinsurance contracts, both in overall terms and in detail.

175. Reinsurance contracts can be complex, and a detailed understanding of individual significant contracts and their inter-relationship with others, as well as an understanding of the programme in total, will be necessary for the auditor to conclude whether the accounting treatment is appropriate and consistent with the substance of the transactions.

176. In addition to considering the controls on the purchasing of reinsurance, the auditor considers the controls exercised by the insurer to ensure that all reinsurance recoveries to which it is entitled have been identified, correctly calculated and collected. As with reinsurance cost, the auditor uses its detailed understanding of the relevant reinsurance contracts to assess whether the appropriate accounting treatment has been followed, particularly for complex reinsurance transactions.

177. An important aspect of the uncertainty to which a particular insurer is exposed is the nature and extent of its reinsurance programme. The auditor considers the nature and coverage of any significant reinsurance programmes and, where material, the procedures adopted by the directors or managing agent to determine the financial stability of reinsurers used. The auditor normally considers the operation of significant reinsurance programmes by reviewing whether the risks ceded and the resulting

premium and expense information are in accordance with the reinsurance contract. The auditor may also consider the procedures in place for ensuring that material claims or balances, if any, disputed by reinsurers are resolved. Evidence may be obtained by reviewing correspondence with reinsurers or intermediaries and considering the quality and timeliness of reconciliations of reinsurer balances.

178. The auditor also uses its understanding of the insurer's reinsurance protection programme to assess the extent to which it is appropriate to recognise credit for reinsurance recoveries within the technical provisions. In its consideration the auditor tests the matching of reinsurance recoveries against gross claims provisions to ensure consistency of treatment.

ISA (UK AND IRELAND) 402: AUDIT CONSIDERATIONS RELATING TO AN ENTITY USING A SERVICE ORGANIZATION

Objective

The objectives of the user auditor, when the user entity uses the services of a service organization, are:

(a) To obtain an understanding of the nature and significance of the services provided by the service organization and their effect on the user entity's internal control relevant to the audit, sufficient to identify and assess the risks of material misstatement; and

(b) To design and perform audit procedures responsive to those risks. (paragraph 7)

When obtaining an understanding of the user entity in accordance with ISA (UK and Ireland) 315, the user auditor shall obtain an understanding of how a user entity uses the services of a service organization in the user entity's operations, including:

(a) The nature of the services provided by the service organization and the significance of those services to the user entity, including the effect thereof on the user entity's internal control;

(b) The nature and materiality of the transactions processed or accounts or financial reporting processes affected by the service organization;

(c) The degree of interaction between the activities of the service organization and those of the user entity; and

(d) The nature of the relationship between the user entity and the service organization, including the relevant contractual terms for the activities undertaken by the service organization.

(e) If the service organisation maintains all or part of a user entity's accounting records, whether those arrangements impact the work the auditor performs to fulfil reporting responsibilities in relation to accounting records that are established in law or regulation. (paragraph 9)

In responding to assessed risks in accordance with ISA (UK and Ireland) 330, the user auditor shall:

(a) Determine whether sufficient appropriate audit evidence concerning the relevant financial statement assertions is available from records held at the user entity; and, if not,

(b) Perform further audit procedures to obtain sufficient appropriate audit evidence or use another auditor to perform those procedures at the service organization on the user auditor's behalf. (paragraph 15)

The user auditor shall modify the opinion in the user auditor's report in accordance with ISA (UK and Ireland) 705 if the user auditor is unable to obtain sufficient appropriate audit evidence regarding the services provided by the service organization relevant to the audit of the user entity's financial statements. (paragraph 20)

179. In common with other industries the outsourcing of functions to service organizations by insurers has become prevalent. Some of the more common areas, such as customer call centres, may have no direct impact on the audit, while others such as IT functions and binding authorities may have a direct relevance. The auditor, therefore, gains an understanding of the extent of outsourced functions and their relevance to the financial statements. The insurer is obliged by SYSC 8.1.8(9) to ensure that the auditor has appropriate access to records, information and explanations from material outsourced operations.

180. Whilst an insurer may outsource functions to service organizations the responsibility for these functions remains that of the insurer. The insurer should have appropriate controls in place over these arrangements including:

- Risk assessment prior to contracting with the service provider, which includes a proper due diligence and periodic review of the appropriateness of the arrangement.

- Appropriate contractual agreements or service level agreements.

- Contingency plans should the provider fail in delivery of services.

- Appropriate management information and reporting from the outsourced provider.

- Appropriate controls over customer information.

181. If the auditor is unable to obtain sufficient appropriate audit evidence concerning outsourced operations the auditor considers whether it is necessary to report the matter direct to the FSA – see the section of this Practice Note relating to ISA (UK and Ireland) 250 Section B.

Additional considerations relating to Lloyd's

182. Many syndicates use the centrally operated systems for clearing underwriting transactions. The auditor of those systems provides an Independent Service Auditor's Report on the operation of those systems each calendar year. A syndicate auditor considers the proposed scope of this work as part of its audit planning process and assesses the level of reliance it intends to place on the work performed

centrally when determining the extent and nature of procedures to be performed at the syndicate.

ISA (UK AND IRELAND) 450: EVALUATION OF MISSTATEMENTS IDENTIFIED DURING THE AUDIT

Objective
The objective of the auditor is to evaluate:

(a) The effect of identified misstatements on the audit; and

(b) The effect of uncorrected misstatements, if any, on the financial statements.
(paragraph 3)

The auditor shall determine whether uncorrected misstatements are material, individually or in aggregate. In making this determination, the auditor shall consider:

(a) The size and nature of the misstatements, both in relation to particular classes of transactions, account balances or disclosures and the financial statements as a whole, and the particular circumstances of their occurrence; ... (paragraph 11)

183. ISA (UK and Ireland) 450 indicates that it may be useful, when evaluating the effect of misstatements accumulated during the audit and communicating misstatements, to distinguish between factual misstatements, judgmental misstatements and projected misstatements. Judgmental misstatements include differences arising from the judgments of management concerning accounting estimates that the auditor considers unreasonable and may therefore include differences arising from the judgments made regarding the calculation of technical provisions. The section of this Practice Note dealing with ISA (UK and Ireland) 540 discusses the evaluation of misstatements within technical provisions.

184. Circumstances which may affect the auditor's evaluation of misstatements include the extent to which the misstatement affects compliance with regulation. Where misstatements which affect compliance with regulation are identified the auditor considers its right and duty to report to regulators in accordance with the section of this Practice Note dealing with ISA (UK & Ireland) 250 Section B.

185. There may be circumstances where the auditor concludes that a classification misstatement is not material in the context of the financial statements as a whole, even though it may exceed the materiality level or levels applied in evaluating other misstatements. For example, a misclassification between balance sheet line items may not be considered material in the context of the financial statements as a whole when the amount of the misclassification is small in relation to the size of the related balance sheet line items and the misclassification does not affect the income statement or any key

ratios. Such qualitative considerations may be relevant when considering certain misstatements in respect of insurers. For example:

- A misstatement of technical provisions may give rise to an offsetting misstatement in reinsurance recoveries to the extent the misstated liabilities have been reinsured.

- A misstatement in respect of revenue from with-profits business may have no direct impact on income where income is determined by the amount of the bonus distribution.

Where liabilities of an insurer are determined directly by reference to the value of assets held (e.g. for unit linked business) any misstatement in such liabilities may be offset by a corresponding misstatement in the associated assets (and vice versa).

ISA (UK AND IRELAND) 500: AUDIT EVIDENCE

Objective

The objective of the auditor is to design and perform audit procedures in such a way as to enable the auditor to obtain sufficient appropriate audit evidence to be able to draw reasonable conclusions on which to base the auditor's opinion. (paragraph 4)

If information to be used as audit evidence has been prepared using the work of a management's expert, the auditor shall, to the extent necessary, having regard to the significance of that expert's work for the auditor's purposes

(a) Evaluate the competence, capabilities and objectivity of that expert;

(b) Obtain an understanding of the work of that expert; and

(c) Evaluate the appropriateness of that expert's work as audit evidence for the relevant assertion. (paragraph 8)

186. In the case of an insurer reporting under UK GAAP undertaking long-term insurance business (other than a Lloyd's corporate member), its Reporting Actuary plays a central role in advising the insurer's board on the determination of the long-term business technical provision disclosed in its financial statements and is likely to be a management's expert. For all insurers, where the work of those with expertise in relation to the actuarial calculation of liabilities is used in the preparation of financial statements then those performing that work are likely to be a management's expert.

187. Where the work of management's actuarial expert is to be used as audit evidence by the auditor of an insurer, the auditor performs the procedures set out in ISA (UK and Ireland) 500 paragraph 8. In performing those procedures the auditor may use an auditor's actuarial expert. The use of auditor's experts is discussed in the section of this Practice Note dealing with ISA (UK and Ireland) 620.

188. In assessing the competence, capability and objectivity of a management's actuarial expert and the appropriateness of that expert's work as audit evidence the auditor has regard to the relevant standards that apply to the expert and its work. In particular, the auditor evaluates the extent to which data used by management's actuarial expert has been derived from sources that have been the subject of audit testing and whether they are the same sources as used by the insurer in preparing the financial statements . In this regard Technical Actuarial Standard D: "Data" requires management's actuarial expert to validate whether "the data is sufficiently accurate, relevant and complete for users to rely on the resulting actuarial information".

ISA (UK AND IRELAND) 505: EXTERNAL CONFIRMATIONS

Objective
The objective of the auditor, when using external confirmation procedures, is to design and perform such procedures to obtain relevant and reliable audit evidence. (paragraph 5)

The auditor shall consider whether external confirmation procedures are to be performed as substantive audit procedures. (paragraph 19 of ISA 330)

189. In general, external confirmation procedures may be useful as part of the audit of:

    (a) Amounts receivable from reinsurers in respect of claims paid or payable by the cedant; and

    (b) Premiums receivable from intermediaries.

    However, external confirmations may not always provide useful audit evidence in relation to insurance balances due to the relative immateriality of individual policyholder balances or transactions.

190. Amounts receivable from reinsurers may comprise an insurer's calculation of amounts that will be recoverable from reinsurers in respect of the insurer's estimate of incurred claims. The relevant reinsurers are unlikely to be in a position to confirm amounts in relation to these claims until such time as the validity of these claims has been assessed, the amounts payable determined, and this has been communicated to and agreed by the relevant reinsurers. Therefore the relevant reinsurers may not be able to provide sufficient appropriate evidence in response to a confirmation request that includes such amounts. The auditor may, however, determine that confirmation would be an effective procedure in respect of individual material reinsurance recoveries where the reinsurer has agreed the amount involved but the balance has not yet been paid.

191. In deciding to what extent to use external confirmations in respect of premiums receivable from intermediaries, the auditor considers the assessed risk of misstatement together with the characteristics of the environment in which the insurer operates and the practice of potential respondents in dealing with requests for direct confirmation. For example where a captive insurer's premium income comprises solely an annual premium from its parent company and this is due at the year-end then this may be a significant balance and it may be assessed that the parent undertaking is likely to be able to respond to a confirmation request. In these circumstances the auditor may decide to seek positive confirmation from the parent undertaking. Conversely, where premiums receivable comprise a high volume of low value amounts which may be due

from individuals or entities that do not have information systems that facilitate external confirmation, the auditor may decide that confirmation may not be an effective audit procedure and may seek to obtain sufficient appropriate evidence from other sources.

ISA (UK AND IRELAND) 520: ANALYTICAL PROCEDURES

Objectives

The objectives of the auditor are:

(a) To obtain relevant and reliable audit evidence when using substantive analytical procedures; and

(b) To design and perform analytical procedures near the end of the audit that assist the auditor when forming an overall conclusion as to whether the financial statements are consistent with the auditor's understanding of the entity. (paragraph 3)

The auditor shall perform risk assessment procedures to provide a basis for the identification and assessment of risks of material misstatement at the financial statement and assertion levels. Risk assessment procedures by themselves, however, do not provide sufficient appropriate audit evidence on which to base the audit opinion. (paragraph 5 of ISA 315)

The risk assessment procedures shall include the following:

(b) Analytical procedures....(paragraph 6 of ISA 315)

192. The deferral and matching principles applied by insurers mean that there are relationships between the movement in balance sheet items and specific items that affect income (for example deferred acquisition costs, claims provisions and unearned premiums provisions).

193. There are likely to be expected relationships between a number of income statement items such as written and earned premiums, incurred claims and earned premiums and premiums and claims gross and reinsurers' share thereof.

194. Given the nature of insurance business, nonfinancial data plays a significant part in managing the pricing and reserving processes. The auditor may consider the usefulness of nonfinancial data such as policy numbers, sums assured, retention levels and claim numbers and their interrelation with financial data in designing analytical review procedures. In addition the auditor may consider measures relating to regulatory compliance – e.g. complaints handling and breaches of conduct of business rules, and operational risk measures – e.g. volumes of unreconciled items.

195. Where nonfinancial information or reports produced from systems or processes outside the financial statements accounting system are used in analytical procedures, the auditor considers the reliability of that information or those reports.

ISA (UK AND IRELAND) 540: AUDITING ACCOUNTING ESTIMATES, INCLUDING FAIR VALUE ACCOUNTING ESTIMATES, AND RELATED DISCLOSURES

Objective

The objective of the auditor is to obtain sufficient appropriate audit evidence about whether:

(a) accounting estimates, including fair value accounting estimates, in the financial statements, whether recognized or disclosed, are reasonable; and

(b) related disclosures in the financial statements are adequate

in the context of the applicable financial reporting framework. (paragraph 6)

When performing risk assessment procedures and related activities to obtain an understanding of the entity and its environment, including the entity's internal control, as required by ISA (UK and Ireland) 315, the auditor shall obtain an understanding of the following in order to provide a basis for the identification and assessment of the risks of material misstatement for accounting estimates:

(a) The requirements of the applicable financial reporting framework relevant to accounting estimates, including related disclosures.

(b) How management identifies those transactions, events and conditions that may give rise to the need for accounting estimates to be recognized or disclosed in the financial statements. In obtaining this understanding, the auditor shall make inquiries of management about changes in circumstances that may give rise to new, or the need to revise existing, accounting estimates.

(c) How management makes the accounting estimates, and an understanding of the data on which they are based, including:

   (i) The method, including where applicable, the model, used in making the accounting estimate;

   (ii) Relevant controls;

   (iii) Whether management has used an expert;

   (iv) The assumptions underlying the accounting estimates;

   (v) Whether there has been or ought to have been a change from the prior period in the methods for making the accounting estimates, and if so, why; and

   (vi) Whether and, if so, how management has assessed the effect of estimation uncertainty. (paragraph 8)

In responding to the assessed risks of material misstatement as required by ISA (UK and Ireland) 330, the auditor shall undertake one or more of the following, taking account of the nature of the accounting estimate:

(a) Determine whether events occurring up to the date of the auditor's report provide audit evidence regarding the accounting estimate.

(b) Test how management made the accounting estimate and the data on which it is based. In doing so, the auditor shall evaluate whether:

   (i) The method of measurement used is appropriate in the circumstances; and

   (ii) The assumptions used by management are reasonable in light of the measurement objectives of the applicable financial reporting framework.

(c) Test the operating effectiveness of the controls over how management made the accounting estimate, together with appropriate substantive procedures.

(d) Develop a point estimate or a range to evaluate management's point estimate. For this purpose:

   (i) If the auditor uses assumptions or methods that differ from management's, the auditor shall obtain an understanding of management's assumptions or methods sufficient to establish that the auditor's point estimate or range takes into account relevant variables and to evaluate any significant differences from management's point estimate.

   (ii) If the auditor concludes that it is appropriate to use a range, the auditor shall narrow the range, based on audit evidence available, until all outcomes within the range are considered reasonable. (paragraph 13)

Technical provisions

196. For most insurers, the estimation of technical provisions will involve relatively high estimation uncertainty because it will involve significant assumptions about future conditions, transactions or events that are uncertain at the time of the estimation. Changes in estimation approach are likely to have a significant effect on the profit figure in the financial statements.

...in responding to the assessed risks of material misstatement in accordance with paragraph 13, the auditor shall consider whether specialized skills or knowledge in relation to one or more aspects of the accounting estimates are required in order to obtain sufficient appropriate audit evidence. (paragraph 14)

197. Audit teams normally involve actuaries in assessing technical provisions. Their level of involvement in the audit process will depend on matters such as the level of expertise of other members of the audit team, the availability of independent actuarial advice to the insurer, and the nature and complexity of the audit issues. They may be used in the initial assessment of the level of risk of each financial statement caption, in assessing the effectiveness of the control environment, in establishing the audit procedures to be adopted and in obtaining and assessing the audit evidence obtained. Further guidance on the use of an actuary is given in the section on ISA (UK and Ireland) 620.

198. When designing audit procedures to test how management made the technical provisions estimate, the auditor obtains an understanding of:

   (a) The policies for setting such provisions;

   (b) The complexity and nature of the models or measurement techniques used to estimate the technical provisions;

   (c) The source data;

   (d) The assumptions used to develop those provisions; and

   (e) Management's controls over the development of technical provisions.

199. Matters that the auditor may consider in obtaining an understanding of relevant controls over how management makes the technical provisions estimate include, for example, the experience and competence of those who make the estimates of the technical provisions, and controls related to:

   • How management determines the completeness, relevance and accuracy of the data used to estimate technical provisions.

   • The review and approval of technical provisions, including the assumptions or inputs used in their development, by appropriate levels of management and, where appropriate, those charged with governance.

   • The segregation of duties between those committing the insurer to the underlying transactions and those responsible for determining technical provisions, including whether the assignment of responsibilities appropriately takes account of the nature of the entity (for example, in the case of a larger insurer, relevant segregation of duties may include an independent function responsible for estimating technical provisions).

   • Where the insurer uses specific models for estimating technical provisions, specific policies and procedures around such models, for example, those established over:

      • The design and development, or selection, of a particular model for a particular purpose.

- The use of the model.

- The maintenance and periodic validation of the integrity of the model.

200. The models used to estimate the technical provisions are dependent upon the accuracy and completeness of financial and non-financial data and accordingly the audit procedures will need to address the effectiveness of management's controls over the use and reliability of such data.

201. The assumptions made by management are integral components of accounting estimates and are intended to provide a reasonable basis for the setting of the technical provisions. The objective of the audit procedures performed for the purpose of evaluating these assumptions is not to obtain sufficient appropriate audit evidence to provide an opinion on the assumptions themselves. Furthermore, the auditor's consideration of management's assumptions is based only on information available to the auditor at the time of the audit. The auditor is not responsible for predicting future conditions, transactions or events that, if they had been known at the time of the audit, might have significantly affected management's actions or management's assumptions underlying the technical provisions and related disclosures. However, the auditor is required to obtain an understanding of the assumptions made by management. Matters that the auditor may consider in obtaining an understanding of the assumptions underlying the accounting estimates include, for example:

- The nature of the assumptions, including which of the assumptions are likely to be significant assumptions.

- How management assesses whether the assumptions are relevant and complete (that is, that all relevant variables have been taken into account).

- Where applicable, how management determines that the assumptions used are internally consistent.

- Whether the assumptions relate to matters within the control of management (for example, assumptions about loss adjustment expenses), and how they conform to the entity's business plans and the external environment, or to matters that are outside its control (for example, assumptions about interest rates, mortality rates, potential judicial or regulatory actions, or the variability and the timing of future cash flows).

- The nature and extent of the documentation, if any, supporting the assumptions.

Assumptions may be made or identified by an expert to assist management in making the technical provisions. Such assumptions, when used by management, become management's assumptions.

202. For life insurers, the realistic valuation of with-profits liabilities uses a range of estimation techniques. The provision will comprise both historic (most likely asset share based) and projected (option and guarantee) information. Options and guarantees are often valued using stochastic modelling techniques. The auditor assesses whether regulatory requirements have been met and whether sufficient scenarios have been run. Any assertions regarding future management and policyholder actions also require careful consideration, including the extent to which management actions are supported by the Principles and Practices of Financial Management (PPFM)[25] or board resolution.

203. Paragraph 52 of Part 2 of Schedule 3 to 2008 Accounts and Reports Regulations provides that the computation of the long-term business provision[26] of a life insurer shall be made by a Fellow of the Institute and Faculty of Actuaries "on the basis of recognised actuarial methods, with due regard to the actuarial principles laid down in Council Directive 2002/83/EC of the European Parliament and of the Council of 5 November 2002 concerning life assurance"[27]. The actuary carrying out this statutory duty for the insurer has been designated as the "Reporting Actuary" by Guidance Note ("GN") 7 "The Role of Actuaries in Relation to Financial Statements of Insurers and Insurance Groups writing Long-term Business and their Relationship with Auditors" issued by The Institute and Faculty of Actuaries and now adopted by the Board for Actuarial Standards (BAS). The statutory duty of the Reporting Actuary[28] does not extend to any technical provisions other than the long-term business provision. The auditor understands the approach which the Reporting Actuary has adopted in calculating the long term business provision.

204. For general insurers there will normally be a range of technical provisions that may be appropriate for inclusion in the financial statements. Guidance Note 12 "General Insurance Business: Actuarial Reports" issued by The Institute and Faculty of Actuaries and adopted by the BAS provides guidance to actuaries on the preparation of a formal

---

25 A document intended to provide information to policyholders and others, in respect of the principles and practices in accordance with which a with-profits fund is managed. The prescribed scope and content of the document are set out in COBS 20.3 in the FSA Handbook.

26 "Long-term business provision" is a term used in Schedule 3 to the 2008 Accounts and Reports Regulations. Insurers preparing financial statements under EU-IFRSs may use different designations for such items. In this Practice Note the term should be interpreted as meaning those items that would fall to be classified as long-term business provisions under Schedule 3 to the 2008 Accounts and Reports Regulations regardless of how they are described in the financial statements. It may be noted that "long-term business provision" in this context does not include provisions in respect of linked long-term contracts.

27 With effect from 1 November 2012 this Directive is repealed and replaced by Directive 2009/138/EC on the "taking up and pursuit of the business of Insurance and Reinsurance (Solvency II)".

28 The statutory duty of a Reporting Actuary arises in Schedule 3 to the 2008 Accounts and Reports Regulations and so does not apply to long-term insurers preparing financial statements under EU-IFRSs, for those companies the term Reporting Actuary in the Practice Note should be taken to refer to any actuary given responsibility by management for the calculation of policyholder liabilities for the purpose of their inclusion in the financial statements.

report on, inter alia, technical provisions or on the financial soundness of a general insurance undertaking[29]. If the actuary has prepared a formal report on the technical provisions or on the financial soundness of a general insurance undertaking the auditor reviews the report to gain a better understanding of the scope of the work performed and of any limitations on any opinions expressed. If such a report has not been prepared, it is necessary for the auditor to understand the scope of the work carried out by the insurer's actuary.

205. Given that the calculation of an insurer's technical provisions is such a significant activity in the preparation of the insurer's financial statements, once management has selected a specific estimation method, it is important that the insurer applies it consistently. If management has changed the method for calculating technical provisions, the auditor considers whether the method to which it has been changed provides a more appropriate basis of measurement, or that the change is supported by a change in the applicable financial reporting framework, or a change in circumstances.

For accounting estimates that give rise to significant risks, in addition to other substantive procedures performed to meet the requirements of ISA (UK and Ireland) 330,[30] the auditor shall evaluate the following:

(a) How management has considered alternative assumptions or outcomes, and why it has rejected them, or how management has otherwise addressed estimation uncertainty in making the accounting estimate.

(b) Whether the significant assumptions used by management are reasonable.

(c) Where relevant to the reasonableness of the significant assumptions used by management or the appropriate application of the applicable financial reporting framework, management's intent to carry out specific courses of action and its ability to do so. (paragraph 15)

206. In obtaining an understanding of whether, and if so how, the insurer has assessed the effect of estimation uncertainty on the technical provisions, the auditor considers matters such as:

- Evaluating how, management has considered alternative assumptions or outcomes and why it has rejected them, or how it has otherwise addressed estimation

---

29 This Guidance Note will be superseded by TAS: Insurance which was issued by BAS on 11 November 2010. The TAS applies to reserved work and work completed for aggregate reports completed after 1 October 2011. The BAS has issued an amended version of GN12 which allows compliance with GN12 by complying with relevant BAS standards.

30 ISA (UK and Ireland) 330, paragraph 18.

uncertainty by, for example, performing a sensitivity analysis to determine the effect of changes in the assumptions on the level of technical provisions.

- How management determines the ultimate technical provisions when analysis indicates that there may be a number of outcome scenarios.

- Whether management monitors the outcome of technical provisions made in the prior period, and whether management has appropriately responded to the outcome of that monitoring procedure.

The auditor shall review the outcome of accounting estimates included in the prior period financial statements, or, where applicable, their subsequent re-estimation for the purpose of the current period. The nature and extent of the auditor's review takes account of the nature of the accounting estimates, and whether the information obtained from the review would be relevant to identifying and assessing risks of material misstatement of accounting estimates made in the current period financial statement. However, the review is not intended to call into question the judgments made in the prior periods that were based on information available at the time. (paragraph 9)

207. The review of the outcome or re-estimation of prior period accounting estimates may assist the auditor in identifying circumstances or conditions that could increase the uncertainty of a technical provision.

The auditor shall review the judgments and decisions made by management in the making of accounting estimates to identify whether there are indicators of possible management bias. Indicators of possible management bias do not themselves constitute misstatements for the purposes of drawing conclusions on the reasonableness of accounting estimates. (paragraph 21)

208. Management bias, whether unintentional or intentional, can be difficult to detect in a particular technical provision. It may only be identified when there has been a change in the method for calculating technical provisions from the prior period based on a subjective assessment without evidence that there has been a change in circumstances when considered in the aggregate of groups of estimates or all estimates, or when observed over a number of accounting periods. Although some form of management bias is inherent in subjective decisions, management may have no intention of misleading the users of financial statements. However, the intentional use by management of accounting estimates which are known to be unreasonable is fraudulent ISA (UK and Ireland) 240, provides standards and guidance on the auditor's responsibility to consider fraud in an audit of financial statements.

The auditor shall obtain sufficient appropriate audit evidence about whether the disclosures in the financial statements related to accounting estimates are in accordance with the requirements of the applicable financial reporting framework. (paragraph 19)

For accounting estimates that give rise to significant risks, the auditor shall also evaluate the adequacy of the disclosure of their estimation uncertainty in the financial statements in the context of the applicable financial reporting framework. (paragraph 20)

209. Insurance specific financial reporting standards, which form part of the applicable financial reporting frameworks for insurers, take into account the inherent uncertainty within the insurance industry and the needs of users of financial statements regarding disclosure of estimation uncertainty. The auditor considers the required disclosure of estimation uncertainty by the applicable financial reporting framework and whether the disclosure proposed by management is adequate. In making this determination, the auditor considers whether adequate disclosure is given regarding the sensitivities associated with the significant assumptions underlying the technical provisions, in light of the materiality level established for the engagement.

210. Insurance specific financial reporting standards can require extensive narrative disclosures in the financial statements of insurers; for example, in relation to the nature and extent of risks arising from insurance contracts and the accounting policies applicable to establishing technical provisions in respect of them. In designing and performing procedures to evaluate these disclosures the auditor obtains audit evidence regarding the assertions about presentation and disclosure described in paragraph A111 of ISA (UK and Ireland) 315. Guidance on the types of audit procedures that can be used for obtaining audit evidence can be found in paragraphs A14 to A25 of ISA (UK and Ireland) 500.

211. Consideration of the adequacy of disclosure with regard to sensitivities of significant assumptions is of particular importance where the estimation uncertainty of technical provisions may cast significant doubt about the entity's ability to continue as a going concern. ISAs (UK and Ireland) 570 and 706 establish standards and provide guidance in such circumstances.

The auditor shall evaluate, based on the audit evidence, whether the accounting estimates in the financial statements are either reasonable in the context of the applicable financial reporting framework, or are misstated. (paragraph 18)

212. Based on the audit evidence obtained, the auditor may conclude that the evidence points to an estimate of the required technical provision that differs from management's estimate, and that the difference between the auditor's estimate or range and management's estimate constitutes a financial statement misstatement. In such cases, where the auditor has developed a range, a misstatement exists when management's estimate lies outside the auditor's range. The misstatement is no less than the difference between management's point estimate and the nearest point of the auditor's range.

Additional considerations relating to Lloyd's

213. The Lloyd's Valuation of Liabilities Rules require all Lloyd's syndicates writing general insurance business to provide to the Council of Lloyd's, each year, for solvency purposes a Statement of Actuarial Opinion (SAO) on their world-wide reserves, both gross and net of reinsurance.

214. The SAO should cover all the business of the syndicate for all years of account from 1993 to date. Separate figures are required gross and net of reinsurance for each year of account. The Institute and Faculty of Actuaries published Guidance Note 20 "Actuarial Reporting Under the Lloyd's Valuation of Liabilities Rules", which has been adopted by the BAS. The actuary's report given in the SAO is limited to an opinion as to whether the reserves for solvency purposes established by the agent comply with the Lloyd's valuation of liability rules and are not less than the expected future costs of the liabilities for claims, net of anticipated future premiums, claims handling expenses and bad debts.

215. In carrying out its work on the syndicate Annual Return, the auditor considers the extent to which it can use the work of the actuary performed for solvency purposes on general insurance business. In making this assessment, the auditor reads the entire SAO and, if available, any related reports; it may also, where appropriate, discuss the contents of the SAO and related reports with the actuary. Factors to be taken into account in assessing the extent of reliance that may be placed on the actuary's work include:

- Any limitations of scope of opinion expressed in the actuary's report.

- The reliability of source data used by the actuary and the adequacy of steps taken by the managing agent to ensure the integrity of that data. Care is necessary to avoid inappropriate reliance if management has supplied data to the actuary, on which reliance has been taken, which has not been considered in the course of the audit of the syndicate's financial statements.

- The extent of any bias in the actuaries' work as a consequence of the actuarial focus being on sufficiency of reserves.

The auditor is also aware that the SAO relates to the solvency reserves of the syndicate for each year of account. The solvency reserves may be different to the technical provisions recorded in the annual report of the syndicate or used in determining the closed year profit or loss.

216. In giving its opinion on the syndicate Annual Return, the syndicate auditor has regard to the appropriateness of the allocation of technical provisions between underlying years of account. In addition, the syndicate auditor has regard to the appropriateness of the determination, and allocation to years of account, of technical provisions to meet FSA solvency requirements. Such provisions must be determined in accordance with requirements prescribed by the FSA and Lloyd's.

217. Where a year of account is closed into a subsequent year of account of the same, or another, syndicate, the Syndicate Accounting Byelaw requires technical provisions of the closed year to be shown as a "premium for a reinsurance to close" (RITC) for that account in the underwriting year accounts as at date of closure. This description has the effect, in accounting terms, of enabling the affairs of that year of account to be drawn to a conclusion and the final result for the relevant annual venture determined. Where the year of account has closed by way of a RITC, the syndicate auditor considers whether, in the context of its opinion on the relevant underwriting year accounts, the relationship between the reinsuring and reinsured members of the syndicate gives rise to further materiality considerations.

218. In situations where the annual venture of a syndicate goes into run off, paragraphs 136-139 of the Insurance SORP are applicable such that provision for any additional costs to be included in a syndicate's annual accounts should be made in the accounting period in which the decision to cease underwriting or not to close a year of account is taken.

219. In order to comply with Lloyd's Solvency criteria, technical provisions for life business included in a syndicate Annual Return must be established and certified by an actuary in a prescribed form on a basis set out by Lloyd's. For solvency purposes, the auditor relies on the life technical provisions established and certified by the actuary.

Derivatives and other financial instruments

...[T]he applicable financial reporting framework may require fair value measurement based on an assumed hypothetical current transaction between knowledgeable, willing parties (sometimes referred to as "marketplace participants" or equivalent) in an arm's length transaction, rather than the settlement of a transaction at some past or future date. (paragraph 3)

THE AUDITING
PRACTICES BOARD

Paragraphs 14, 18 and 21 of ISA (UK and Ireland) 540 which are reproduced in the technical provisions section above are also relevant to estimates relating to derivatives and other financial instruments.

220. The valuation of derivative and other financial instruments which are not traded in an active market and so for which valuation techniques are required is an activity that can give rise to significant audit risk. Such financial instruments are priced using valuation techniques such as discounted cash flow models, options pricing models or by reference to another instrument that is substantially the same as the financial instrument subject to valuation. The auditor reviews the controls, procedures and testing of the valuation techniques used by the insurer. Controls and substantive testing could include focusing on:

- Valuation technique approval and testing procedures used by the insurer.

- The independence of review, sourcing and reasonableness of observable market data and other parameters used in the valuation techniques.

- Calibration procedures used by the insurer to test the validity of valuation techniques applied by comparing outputs to observable market transactions.

- Completeness and appropriate inclusion of all relevant observable market data.

- The observability in practice of data classified by the insurer as observable market data.

- The appropriateness and validity of classification of instruments designated as being traded in a non active and in an active market.

- The appropriateness and validity of the particular valuation technique applied to particular financial instruments.

- The appropriateness and validity of the parameters used by the insurer to designate an instrument as substantially the same as the financial instrument being valued.

- Mathematical integrity of the valuation models.

- Access controls over valuation models.

221. In the more subjective areas of valuation the auditor obtains an understanding of the assumptions used and undertakes a review of the estimates involved for reasonableness, consistency and conformity with generally accepted practices. In some cases, the auditor may use its own valuation techniques to assess the insurer's valuations. Given the complexities involved and the subjective nature of the judgments inherent the auditor may involve an expert in elements of this work (see the ISA (UK and Ireland) 620 section of this Practice Note). Further guidance on auditing complex

financial instruments is provided in the APB's Practice Note 23 "Auditing complex financial instruments (Revised)".

> The auditor shall obtain sufficient appropriate audit evidence about whether the disclosures in the financial statements related to accounting estimates are in accordance with the requirements of the applicable financial reporting framework. (paragraph 19)
>
> For accounting estimates that give rise to significant risks, the auditor shall also evaluate the adequacy of the disclosures of their estimation uncertainty in the financial statements in the context of the applicable financial reporting framework. (paragraph 20)

222. In designing and performing procedures to evaluate disclosures relating to derivative and other financial instruments the auditor obtains audit evidence regarding the assertions about presentation and disclosure as discussed in paragraph A111(c) of ISA (UK and Ireland) 315. Guidance on the types of audit procedures that can be used for obtaining audit evidence can be found in paragraphs A14 to A25 of ISA (UK and Ireland) 500.

ISA (UK AND IRELAND) 550: RELATED PARTIES

Objectives

The objectives of the auditor are:

(a) Irrespective of whether the applicable financial reporting framework establishes related party requirements, to obtain an understanding of related party relationships and transactions sufficient to be able:

  (i) To recognize fraud risk factors, if any, arising from related party relationships and transactions that are relevant to the identification and assessment of the risks of material misstatement due to fraud; and

  (ii) To conclude, based on the audit evidence obtained, whether the financial statements, insofar as they are affected by those relationships and transactions

    a. Achieve fair presentation (for fair presentation frameworks); or

    b. Are not misleading (for compliance frameworks); and

(b) In addition, where the applicable financial reporting framework establishes related party requirements, to obtain sufficient appropriate audit evidence about whether related party relationships and transactions have been appropriately identified, accounted for and disclosed in the financial statements in accordance with the framework. (paragraph 9)

In meeting the ISA (UK and Ireland) 315 requirement to identify and assess the risks of material misstatement, the auditor shall identify and assess the risks of material misstatement associated with related party relationships and transactions and determine whether any of those risks are significant risks. In making this determination, the auditor shall treat identified significant related party transactions outside the entity's normal course of business as giving rise to significant risks. (paragraph 18)

223. The auditor is required to assess the risk that material undisclosed related party transactions may exist. It is in the nature of insurance business that transaction volumes are high but this factor will not, of itself, necessarily lead the auditor to conclude that the inherent risk of material undisclosed related party transactions is high.

224. Insurers are likely to have a particularly wide range of contractual arrangements because the nature of insurance is to spread risk. The directors will, in particular, need to consider how best to obtain information on the interests of related parties in policies issued and in reinsurance arrangements. In capturing this data, insurers may decide to establish criteria for evaluating materiality to the individuals concerned; the policies are, in most

cases, unlikely to be material to the insurer. The auditor will need to obtain an understanding of the controls that management has established to identify, account for and disclose such related party transactions.

225. Insurers are required to report to the FSA changes in control (in some instances with FSA prior approval), changes in circumstances of existing controllers and changes in entities that are closely linked to the firm (SUP 11). In addition, there are annual reporting obligations in respect of controllers and entities that are closely linked to the firm (SUP 16). As a result, it will therefore normally be the case that there are controls in place to ensure that this information is properly collated. However, the definition of "controller and closely linked" for regulatory purposes is not congruent with the "related party" definition in FRS 8/IAS 24 and the auditor therefore considers what controls have been put in place by management to capture information on those parties which fall within the accounting definition only.

226. In reviewing related party information for completeness, the auditor may compare the proposed disclosures in the financial statements to information prepared for regulatory reporting purposes (bearing in mind that the population may be different, as noted in the preceding paragraph).

For identified significant related party transactions outside the entity's normal course of business, the auditor shall:

(a) Inspect the underlying contracts or agreements, if any, and evaluate whether:

  (i)   The business rationale (or lack thereof) of the transactions suggests that they may have been entered into to engage in fraudulent financial reporting or to conceal misappropriation of assets;

  (ii) The terms of the transactions are consistent with management's explanations; and

  (iii) The transactions have been appropriately accounted for and disclosed in accordance with the applicable financial reporting framework; and

(b) Obtain audit evidence that the transactions have been appropriately authorized and approved. (paragraph 23)

227. The auditor inspects, evaluates and obtains audit evidence regarding the authorisation and approval of and significant reinsurance or other funding arrangements with related parties entered into outside the entity's normal course of business. In gaining an understanding of the business rationale of such transactions that auditor makes appropriate enquiries of management.

ISA (UK AND IRELAND) 560: SUBSEQUENT EVENTS

Objectives
The objectives of the auditor are:

(a) To obtain sufficient appropriate audit evidence about whether events occurring between the date of the financial statements and the date of the auditor's report that require adjustment of, or disclosure in, the financial statements are appropriately reflected in those financial statements in accordance with the applicable financial reporting framework; and

(b) To respond appropriately to facts that become known to the auditor after the date of the auditor's report that, had they been known to the auditor at that date, may have caused the auditor to amend the auditor's report. (paragraph 4)

The auditor shall perform audit procedures designed to obtain sufficient appropriate audit evidence that all events occurring between the date of the financial statements and the date of the auditor's report that require adjustment of, or disclosure in, the financial statements have been identified. The auditor is not, however, expected to perform additional audit procedures on matters to which previously applied audit procedures have provided satisfactory conclusions. (paragraph 6)

228. Matters specific to insurance companies which the auditor may consider in its review of subsequent events include:

- An evaluation of the impact of any material subsequent events on the capital resources requirement for the insurer.

- An assessment of the influence of new information received relevant to claims provisions.

- An assessment of the impact of any developments in doubtful reinsurance recoveries since the balance sheet date.

- An assessment of the impact of any regulatory developments since the balance sheet date.

- A review of relevant correspondence with regulators and enquiries of management to determine whether any significant breaches of regulations or other significant regulatory concerns have come to light since the period end.

229. ISA (UK and Ireland) 560 establishes requirements for situations when facts become known to the auditor:

(a) After the date of the auditor's report but before the financial statements are issued; and

(b) After the financial statements have been issued

that may have caused the auditor to amend the auditor's report. If the auditor examines the regulatory return of an insurer subsequent to the issuance of its report on the financial statements, the auditor may become aware of subsequent events which, had they occurred or been known of at the date of its report on the financial statements, might have caused the auditor to issue a different report. In such cases the auditor and the directors consider whether the financial statements need to be revised following the statutory provisions relating to the revision of company annual financial statements and directors' reports set out in section 454 of CA 2006 and The Companies (Revision of Defective Accounts and Reports) Regulations 2008. Where the auditor concludes that this step is appropriate, the matter concerned is likely to be of material significance to the FSA and so give rise to a duty to report to the FSA.

Additional considerations relating to Lloyd's

230. Currently the syndicate Annual Return is required to be submitted to Lloyd's before the syndicate annual accounts are issued. If there has been a post-balance sheet event after the syndicate Annual Return has been signed but before the syndicate annual accounts and (where relevant) personal accounts are signed which is of such significance that it materially affects the view shown in these accounts, then they should be amended. Lloyd's rules may require that an amendment is also made to the syndicate Annual Return. Paragraph 228 sets out matters specific to insurance companies that the auditor may consider in its review of subsequent events. The evaluation of the impact of any material event on the capital resources requirement of the insurer is not applicable to the audit of syndicate accounts. Accordingly, other matters that the auditor may consider in its review of subsequent events include an evaluation of the impact of any material subsequent events on the syndicate's ability to continue to write business in the current annual venture or annual ventures yet to be established for subsequent years.

ISA (UK AND IRELAND) 570: GOING CONCERN

Objectives

The objectives of the auditor are:

(a) To obtain sufficient appropriate audit evidence regarding the appropriateness of management's use of the going concern assumption in the preparation of the financial statements;

(b) To conclude, based on the audit evidence obtained, whether a material uncertainty exists related to events or conditions that may cast significant doubt on the entity's ability to continue as a going concern; and

(c) To determine the implications for the auditor's report. (paragraph 9)

If the auditor concludes that the use of the going concern assumption is appropriate in the circumstances but a material uncertainty exists, the auditor shall determine whether the financial statements:

(a) Adequately describe the principal events or conditions that may cast significant doubt on the entity's ability to continue as a going concern and management's plans to deal with these events or conditions; and

(b) Disclose clearly that there is a material uncertainty related to events or conditions that may cast significant doubt on the entity's ability to continue as a going concern and, therefore, that it may be unable to realize its assets and discharge its liabilities in the normal course of business. (paragraph 18)

231. With reference to insurance companies, specific audit procedures may include:

- Reviewing the means whereby the board of directors and senior management of an insurer satisfy themselves that the insurer will have capital in excess of its capital resources requirement for the foreseeable future, including a review of the insurer's Individual Capital Assessment prepared for regulatory purposes.

- Considering whether the key assumptions underlying the budgets and/or forecasts appear appropriate in the circumstances. Key assumptions will normally include claims projections (numbers, cost and timing), the profitability of business written and the level of provisions required.

- Considering the liquidity of funds to enable the insurer to meet claims and other liabilities as they fall due.

- Reviewing correspondence with the regulators, and considering any actions taken (or likely to be taken) by the regulators.

- Considering the potential costs of settling claims, (for example uncertainty resulting from judicial decisions) and additional provisions (for example product mis-selling).

- For a life insurer, reviewing any financial condition report produced by the holder of the actuarial function and other actuarial reports.

If the auditor has any doubts as to the ability of an insurer to continue as a going concern, the auditor considers whether it ought to make a report direct to the FSA on which guidance is set out in the section of this Practice Note relating to ISA (UK and Ireland) 250 Section B.

Additional considerations relating to Lloyd's

232. The managing agent's responsibility for preparing syndicate annual accounts includes the requirement for the financial statements to be prepared on the basis that the syndicate will continue to write future business unless it is inappropriate to presume the syndicate will do so. Syndicate annual accounts present the collective participations of the members of the syndicate in one or more annual ventures. The ability of a syndicate to meet its obligations as they fall due will reflect the ability of the members of the syndicate to meet their obligations to the syndicate when calls are made. However, irrespective of whether information on a syndicate member's ability to meet its obligations as they fall due is available, the ability of a syndicate to meet its obligations as they fall due is underpinned by the support provided by Lloyd's solvency process and its chain of security for any syndicate members who are unable to meet their underwriting liabilities.

233. Unless it is in run-off, at the date the annual accounts are approved the syndicate will have commenced underwriting business through Lloyd's for the new underwriting year, but it will not have established an annual venture for subsequent years. Accordingly, it is not necessary to carry out some of the audit procedures set out in paragraph 231; in particular an assessment of the available capital resources is not applicable to syndicate annual accounts. However, audit procedures include making enquiries of the managing agent on the plans for the underwriting of business in future annual ventures of the syndicate.

ISA (UK AND IRELAND) 580: WRITTEN REPRESENTATIONS

Objectives

The objectives of the auditor are:

(a) To obtain written representations from management and, where appropriate, those charged with governance that they believe that they have fulfilled their responsibility for the preparation of the financial statements and for the completeness of the information provided to the auditor;

(b) To support other audit evidence relevant to the financial statements or specific assertions in the financial statements by means of written representations if determined necessary by the auditor or required by other ISAs (UK and Ireland); and

(c) To respond appropriately to written representations provided by management and, where appropriate, those charged with governance, or if management or, where appropriate, those charged with governance do not provide the written representations requested by the auditor. (paragraph 6)

The auditor shall request written representations from management with appropriate responsibilities for the financial statements and knowledge of the matters concerned. (paragraph 9)

Other ISAs (UK and Ireland) require the auditor to request written representations. If, in addition to such required representations, the auditor determines that it is necessary to obtain one or more written representations to support other audit evidence relevant to the financial statements or one or more specific assertions in the financial statements the auditor shall request such other written representations. (paragraph 13)

---

234. ISAs (UK and Ireland) 250 Section A and 550 require the auditor to obtain written confirmation in respect of:

(a) The completeness of disclosure to the auditor of all known instances of non-compliance or suspected non-compliance with laws and regulations (including breaches of FSMA 2000, FSA rules, the Money Laundering Regulations, other regulatory requirements or any other circumstance that could jeopardise the authorisation of the firm under FSMA 2000) whose effects should be considered when preparing financial statements *(paragraph 16 ISA (UK and Ireland)250 Section A)*; and

(b) The completeness of information provided regarding the identity of related parties, related party relationships and transactions, and the appropriateness of related party disclosures in the financial statements *(paragraph 26 ISA (UK and Ireland)) 550.*

235. If, in addition to the requirements in other ISAs (UK and Ireland) for the auditor to request written representations, the auditor determines that it is necessary to obtain one or more written representations to support other audit evidence relevant to the financial statements or specific assertions this ISA (UK and Ireland) requires that the auditor shall request such other written representations. For life insurers falling within the FSA's realistic capital regime, representations in relation to the management actions assumed in the valuation of realistic liabilities are likely to be relevant. For all insurers, it may be appropriate to obtain a specific representation confirming that full disclosure has been made in respect of any side letters, any multiyear reinsurance contracts or any reinsurance contracts with unusual adjustable features, as well as the adequacy of the claims provision and the IBNR. The auditor may also obtain written representations regarding, for example:

- The reasonableness of significant assumptions used by the entity in calculating technical provisions.

- All correspondence with regulators having been made available to the auditor.

ISA (UK AND IRELAND) 600: SPECIAL CONSIDERATIONS – AUDITS OF GROUP FINANCIAL STATEMENTS (INCLUDING THE WORK OF COMPONENT AUDITORS)

Objectives

The objectives of the auditor are:

(a) To determine whether to act as the auditor of the group financial statements; and

(b) If acting as the auditor of the group financial statements:

    (i) To communicate clearly with component auditors about the scope and timing of their work on financial information related to components and their findings; and

    (ii) To obtain sufficient appropriate audit evidence regarding the financial information of the components and the consolidation process to express an opinion on whether the group financial statements are prepared, in all material respects, in accordance with the applicable financial reporting framework. (paragraph 8)

The group engagement partner is responsible for the direction, supervision and performance of the group audit engagement in compliance with professional standards and applicable legal and regulatory requirements and whether the auditor's report that is issued is appropriate in the circumstances. As a result, the auditor's report on the group financial statements shall not refer to a component auditor, unless required by law or regulation to include such reference. If such reference is required by law or regulation, the auditor's report shall indicate that the reference does not diminish the group engagement partner's or the group engagement partner's firm's responsibility for the group audit opinion. (paragraph 11)

If the group engagement team plans to request a component auditor to perform work on the financial information of a component, the group engagement team shall obtain an understanding of the following:

(a) Whether the component auditor understands and will comply with the ethical requirements that are relevant to the group audit and, in particular, is independent.

(b) The component auditor's professional competence.

(c) Whether the group engagement team will be able to be involved in the work of the component auditor to the extent necessary to obtain sufficient appropriate audit evidence.

(d) Whether the component auditor operates in a regulatory environment that actively oversees auditors. (paragraph 19)

236. The auditor considers in particular the competence and capability of the component auditor having regard to the laws, regulation and industry practice relevant to the component to be reported on by the component auditor and, where relevant, whether the component auditor has access to actuarial or other expertise appropriate to the component's insurance business.

237. Further procedures may be necessary for the auditor of a UK insurer where audit work in support of the audit opinion is undertaken by an individual or audit firm that is not subject to the UK audit regulatory regime. Where an overseas firm of the auditor (or an audit firm independent of the auditor) is undertaking audit procedures on a branch, or division or in-house shared service centre of the insurer, the auditor has due regard to the requirements in the Audit Regulations[31] to ensure all relevant members of the engagement team are and continue to be fit and proper, are and continue to be competent and are aware of and follow the Audit Regulations and any related procedures and requirements established by the audit firm. This includes the auditor's duty to report direct to the FSA in certain circumstances – see ISA (UK and Ireland) 250 Section B.

238. In rare circumstances a branch or other part of a UK authorised insurer may be audited by another firm. In these circumstances the component auditor has a duty to report matters of material significance to the FSA rather than via the auditor of the authorised insurer. However, it is likely that any such matters would have a direct bearing on the work of the auditor of the authorised insurer and would likely be reported to its auditor. In such circumstances the auditor of the authorised insurer would consider also reporting such matters directly to the FSA. More detailed consideration of the auditor's duty to report to the FSA is set out in the section of this Practice Note dealing with ISA (UK and Ireland) 250 Section B.

Additional considerations relating to Lloyd's

Lloyd's corporate members

239. Lloyd's has established a central facility to assist corporate members in preparing their statutory financial statements. The facility accumulates information from underlying syndicates and then calculates and aggregates each corporate member's share of that information. The syndicate information is provided to Lloyd's within the syndicate Annual Return together with a syndicate auditor's report thereon.

240. Where corporate members rely on information provided by way of the central facility, the auditor of corporate members applies the principles of ISA (UK and Ireland) 600

---

31 Audit Regulations and Guidelines – 2008 issued by the Institute of Chartered Accountants in England and Wales, the Institute of Chartered Accountants of Scotland and the Institute of Chartered Accountants in Ireland.

in considering how the work of syndicate auditors affects its audit. Where the auditor of corporate members relies on the work of syndicate auditors, it considers the professional qualifications, experience and resources of the other auditors in the context of its audit of the corporate member in question. It obtains appropriate evidence that the work of the syndicate auditors is sufficient for the purposes of the audit of the corporate member's financial statements.

Lloyd's syndicates

241. The auditor of a syndicate frequently experiences situations where audit evidence is derived from information audited by other auditors, for example, where the audit of the managing agent is carried out by a separate firm from the syndicate's auditor. Consequently, the syndicate's auditor may have regard to the work of the agency's auditor, for example, in respect of recharged expenses. Similarly, in the case of certain service company activities on behalf of the syndicate, the syndicate auditor may have regard to the work of the auditor of the service company.

ISA (UK AND IRELAND) 620: USING THE WORK OF AN AUDITOR'S EXPERT[32]

Objectives

The objectives of the auditor are:

(a) To determine whether to use the work of an auditor's expert; and

(b) If using the work of an auditor's expert, to determine whether that work is adequate for the auditor's purpose. (paragraph 5)

The auditor shall evaluate the adequacy of the auditor's expert's work for the auditor's purposes including:

(a) The relevance and reasonableness of that expert's findings or conclusions, and their consistency with other audit evidence;

(b) If that expert's work involves use of significant assumptions and methods, the relevance and reasonableness of those assumptions and methods in the circumstances; and

(c) If that expert's work involves the use of source data that is significant to that expert's work, the relevance, completeness, and accuracy of that source data. (paragraph 12)

242. Expertise in a field other than accounting or auditing may include expertise in relation to the actuarial calculation of liabilities associated with insurance contracts. As stated in the section on ISA (UK and Ireland) 540, given the nature and complexity of insurance business the auditor may use an actuary in assessing technical provisions in the audit of the financial statements. IPRU(INS) requires the auditor of a life insurer to obtain and pay due regard to the advice of a Reviewing Actuary when reporting on regulatory returns (see "Reporting on regulatory returns" section). Where the auditor uses an auditor's expert, such as an actuary, as part of the audit, the auditor remains solely responsible for the audit of the insurer's financial statements and will not refer to the work of the auditor's expert within the auditor's report.

243. Where the auditor decides to use an actuary as an auditor's expert in relation to the audit of technical provisions, the auditor assesses the following:

(a) The professional competence and capabilities of the actuary, taking into consideration its professional qualifications, experience and reputation in the market in which the insurer operates;

---

32 The applicable quality control standards and guidance relating to a person using expertise in a specialized area of accounting or auditing are those set out in ISA (UK and Ireland) 220.

THE AUDITING
PRACTICES BOARD

(b) The objectivity of the actuary including whether the actuary is connected in some way to the insurer e.g. being financially dependent on the insurer or having a financial interest in the insurer; and

(c) The scope of the work to be undertaken and degree of reliance that the auditor can place thereon.

The auditor seeks to ensure that an actuary engaged as an auditor's expert, although guided by its own profession's standards and guidance and by BAS technical standards (TASs), designs and performs its work to provide the auditor with work that fully meets the objectives agreed between the auditor and the actuary.

244. Where the actuary is an internal expert (i.e. a partner or staff, including temporary staff, of the auditor's firm or a network firm), the auditor (unless information provided to the auditor suggests otherwise) will be able to rely on its firm's quality control systems, recruitment and training to determine the actuary's capabilities and competence, rather than having to evaluate them for each audit engagement.

245. Regardless of whether the actuary is an auditor's internal or external expert, ISA (UK and Ireland) 620 requires the auditor to agree with the actuary:

(a) The nature, scope and objectives of the actuary's work.

(b) The respective roles and responsibilities of the auditor and the actuary;

(c) The nature, timing and extent of communication between the auditor and the actuary, including the form of any report to be provided by the actuary; and

(d) The need for the actuary to observe confidentiality requirements.

Where appropriate, such agreement is in writing. An agreement between the auditor and an auditor's external actuarial expert will often be in the form of an engagement letter. See paragraph 50, in the section on ISA 230, for further guidance on documentation.

246. In addition the auditor may wish to arrange to have access to the working papers produced by any actuary who is an auditor's external expert. The working papers of an actuary who is an auditor's internal expert form part of the audit documentation.

247. The auditor evaluates the actuary's working papers to determine whether:

(a) The actuary's findings are relevant and reasonable, based on the auditor's knowledge of the business and the results of other audit procedures;

(b) The methods and assumptions used by the actuary are relevant and reasonable in the circumstances; and

(c) The source data used by the actuary is relevant, reasonable, complete and accurate.

Although the auditor does not have the same expertise as the actuary this does not preclude the auditor from challenging the actuary's findings.

248. If the actuary's findings are not consistent with other audit evidence, the auditor attempts to resolve the differences by either agreeing with the actuary on the nature and extent of further work to be performed by the actuary or by applying additional audit procedures. If the auditor is not satisfied that it has obtained sufficient appropriate audit evidence to support the audit opinion and there is no satisfactory alternative source of audit evidence, the auditor considers the implications for the auditor's report.

ISA (UK AND IRELAND) 700: THE AUDITOR'S REPORT ON FINANCIAL STATEMENTS

Objectives

The objectives of the auditor are to:

(a) Form an opinion on the financial statements based on an evaluation of the conclusions drawn from the audit evidence obtained; and

(b) Express clearly that opinion through a written report that also describes the basis for the opinion. (paragraph 7)

With respect to true and fair frameworks an unqualified opinion on the financial statements shall be expressed only when the auditor concludes that they have been prepared in accordance with the identified financial reporting framework, including the requirements of applicable law, and the financial statements give a true and fair view. (paragraph 11)

Equalisation provisions

249. INSPRU 1.4 sets out the type of general insurance business in respect of which equalisation provisions are required to be established and maintained by authorised insurers and the formulae to be used in calculating the amount of such provisions.

250. Whilst not permitted under EU-IFRSs, for general insurers preparing financial statements in accordance with UK GAAP, Schedule 3 to the 2008 Accounts and Reports Regulations requires equalisation provisions to be included in an authorised insurer's balance sheet as part of "technical provisions" under the general heading "liabilities" (Balance sheet format, item C5 and paragraph 56 of Schedule 3 to the Regulations). However such equalisation provisions, although required by law, are not "liabilities" as normally defined for the purposes of accounting standards. Consequently, the APB has taken legal advice to clarify the position. The advice obtained is to the following effect:

Individual authorised insurers:

(a) Individual authorised insurers are required by statute to include equalisation provisions in financial statements prepared in accordance with the 2008 Accounts and Reports Regulations; and

(b) The statutory regime does not permit an argument that, in the generality of cases, the inclusion of equalisation provisions would be inconsistent with showing a true and fair view;

Insurance groups:

(a) Any equalisation provisions in the financial statements of those undertakings being consolidated should be included in the consolidated financial statements;

(b) Such equalisation provisions may not in the generality of cases:

   (i) Be excluded from the consolidated financial statements to ensure that those statements conform with generally accepted accounting principles or practice (Schedule 6 of the 2008 Accounts and Reports Regulations, paragraphs 1(1), 31 and 32; or

   (ii) Be adjusted so as to accord with the rules used for the group financial statements (Schedule 6 of the 2008 Accounts and Reports Regulations, paragraph 3(1)); or

   (iii) Be excluded on the basis that, under section 404 of CA 2006, the inclusion of such equalisation provisions in the consolidated financial statements would be inconsistent with showing a true and fair view; and

(c) It would not be appropriate, with the objective of ensuring that accounting policies shall be applied consistently within the same financial statements:

   (i) To include, on consolidation, equalisation provisions in respect of the businesses of those undertakings which are not required by law to establish equalisation provisions; or

   (ii) To eliminate all equalisation provisions in the consolidated financial statements.

The legal advice did not extend to the case of individual authorised insurers or groups preparing their financial statements in accordance with EU-IFRSs. However, where this is the case equalisation provisions should not be included in the balance sheet.

251. The Insurance SORP recommends that financial statements incorporating equalisation provisions should disclose:

(a) That the amounts provided are in addition to the provisions required to meet the anticipated ultimate cost of settlement of outstanding claims at the balance sheet date, and that notwithstanding this, Schedule 3 to the 2008 Accounts and Reports Regulations requires the amounts to be included within technical provisions; and

(b) The impact of equalisation provisions on shareholders' funds and the effect of movements in the provisions on the results of the accounting period (and, if appropriate, an alternative earnings per share figure disregarding equalisation provisions).

252. Provided that adequate disclosure is made in financial statements which contain statutory equalisation provisions (and in the absence of other reasons to conclude that

the financial statements do not give a true and fair view), it is appropriate to regard the financial statements incorporating such equalisation provisions as giving, in the particular circumstances, the required true and fair view. Consequently, unless special circumstances exist which are particular to the insurer concerned, the auditor is justified in concluding that financial statements including such provisions give a true and fair view, and in expressing an unqualified opinion to that effect.

253. Such an unqualified opinion is only appropriate if:

(a) The provisions are established in accordance with the statutory requirements; and

(b) The financial statements include adequate disclosure concerning the provisions.

254. Factors which need to be taken into account in forming a judgment on the adequacy of disclosure include:

- Whether the amounts concerned are clearly distinguished from other items in technical provisions.

- Whether the reasons for the effects of the accounting treatment followed are adequately described such that a reader would appreciate the special nature of the provisions.

- Whether the disclosure includes comment making it clear that the amounts so included in liabilities are over and above the provisions required to meet the anticipated ultimate cost of settlement of outstanding claims at the balance sheet date.

- Whether a reader is able to identify the financial effect of equalisation provisions on the insurer's net assets and the effect of movements in the provisions on the results for the period.

255. When the effect of equalisation provisions is material to the financial statements and an unqualified opinion is expressed, it is appropriate for the auditor to include reference to the legal requirements governing equalisation provisions in the introductory paragraph to the auditor's report as part of the description of the financial reporting framework that has been applied in the preparation of the financial statements. Illustrative wording of such an introductory paragraph is set out in the example auditor's report in Example 17 in Bulletin 2010/2.

Additional considerations relating to Lloyd's

256. The auditor of a Lloyd's syndicate's financial statements is required to report its opinion as to whether the annual accounts comply with the requirements of the 2008 Lloyd's Regulations. Where syndicate underwriting year accounts are prepared for a

run-off year of account, the auditor is required to report its opinion as to whether those accounts comply with the requirements of the Syndicate Accounting Byelaw.

257. In addition, its report on the annual accounts includes its opinion on whether they give a true and fair view of the calendar year result and of the state of affairs at the balance sheet date. The report of the auditor on closed year underwriting year accounts includes its opinion on whether they give a true and fair view of the result of the closed year of account.

258. Lloyd's require that the auditor's report on syndicate underwriting year accounts be addressed to the members of the syndicate participating in the year of account to which they relate and not to all members of the syndicate. Different reporting requirements apply to syndicate underwriting year accounts for a closed year of account as apply to syndicate underwriting year accounts for a run-off year of account which is not closing.

259 Syndicates are not permitted to maintain equalisation provisions.

260. In preparing underwriting accounts for a closed year of a syndicate, compliance with UK GAAP is normally necessary in order to give a true and fair view of the syndicate's closed year result.

261. Inherent uncertainty is also relevant to syndicate underwriting year accounts.

An auditor reporting on underwriting accounts, therefore, considers whether:

(a) The accounts have been prepared on an appropriate basis;

(b) Appropriate disclosures have been made; and

(c) Any uncertainties are significant, having regard to the types of business underwritten by the syndicate.

If the auditor is required to report on certain matters by exception the auditor shall describe its responsibilities under the heading "Matters on which we are required to report by exception" and incorporate a suitable conclusion in respect of such matters. (paragraph 22)

262. The auditor of a syndicate's annual and underwriting year accounts is required to report by exception if:

(a) The managing agent has not maintained proper accounting records in respect of the syndicate;

(b) The underwriting year accounts do not agree with the accounting records; and the auditor of the syndicate's annual accounts is additionally required to report by exception if

(c) It has not received all the information and explanations that it requires.

Illustrative wording of an auditor's report on the annual accounts is provided in Example 18 of Bulletin 2010/2 and on underwriting accounts in Examples 19 and 20 of Bulletin 2010/2.

Members' personal accounts (including syndicate MAPA accounts)

263. Managing agents are required to prepare personal accounts and MAPA accounts where there is a closed and/or run-off year of account of a syndicate if they are required to prepare syndicate underwriting year accounts or run-off accounts. In addition to its report on a syndicate's annual accounts and underwriting year accounts, a syndicate auditor is required to report as to whether the managing agent's procedures and controls provide assurance that:

(a) Members' personal accounts and syndicate MAPA accounts have been properly prepared in accordance with the Syndicate Accounting Byelaw; and

(b) The net results shown in members' personal accounts and syndicate MAPA accounts have been calculated in accordance with the applicable agency agreements.

In order to be in a position to express an opinion that the procedures and controls taken as a whole are adequate to enable the managing agent to comply with the provisions of the Lloyd's Syndicate Accounting Byelaw, a syndicate auditor considers the need for additional procedures beyond those undertaken for the audit of the annual accounts and of the underwriting accounts. Illustrative wording of such a report is shown in example 1.5 of Appendix 1.

264. In providing support for its opinion on members' personal accounts a syndicate auditor obtains an understanding of management's process for the preparation of accounts of individual Lloyd's syndicate members and identifies, and tests as appropriate, the controls that management have established to ensure they are operating effectively. Management controls will include controls to ensure that:

- Records of individual Lloyd's syndicate participations are accurately maintained.

- Changes in Lloyd's reporting requirements in respect of personal accounts are identified and, if necessary, systems are updated.

- Personal account totals are reconciled with syndicate accounting records.

- Output from the system is monitored to ensure that Lloyd's requirements have been complied with.

265. An auditor of personal accounts is required to report by exception if:

(a) The managing agent has not maintained proper accounting records in respect of the syndicate;

(b) The personal accounts do not agree with the accounting records; and

(c) It has not received all the information and explanations that it requires.

ISA (UK AND IRELAND) 705: MODIFICATIONS TO OPINIONS IN THE INDEPENDENT AUDITOR'S REPORT

Objective
The objective of the auditor is to express clearly an appropriately modified opinion on the financial statements that is necessary when:

(a) The auditor concludes, based on the audit evidence obtained, that the financial statements as a whole are not free from material misstatement; or

(b) The auditor is unable to obtain sufficient appropriate audit evidence to conclude that the financial statements as a whole are free from material misstatement. (paragraph 4)

When the auditor modifies the opinion on the financial statements, the auditor shall, in addition to the specific elements required by ISA (UK and Ireland) 700, include a paragraph in the auditor's report that provides a description of the matter giving rise to the modification. The auditor shall place this paragraph immediately before the opinion paragraph in the auditor's report and use the heading "Basis for Qualified Opinion," "Basis for Adverse Opinion." or "Basis for Disclaimer of Opinion," as appropriate. (paragraph 16)

266. The basis on which an insurer's financial statements are prepared takes account of the extent of the inherent uncertainty in the types of insurance business it underwrites. Uncertainties arising from insurance contracts may include:

- General uncertainties arising where the outcomes for provisioning are within a range which is not unusual for the nature of the business underwritten.

- Specific uncertainties which are material and subject to a very wide range of outcomes.

- Uncertainties where the financial reporting framework does not require a provision to be established but where disclosure of a contingent liability may be appropriate.

267. If the auditor concludes that the technical provisions are materially misstated or that the disclosures relating to those provisions and the relevant uncertainties are inadequate or misleading and concludes that the effect is material, but not pervasive, to the view given by the financial statements, it is required to express a qualified opinion.

268. If the auditor concludes that the effect is both material and pervasive it is required to express an adverse opinion. If the auditor is unable to obtain sufficient appropriate audit evidence on which to base an opinion, and the auditor concludes that the possible

effects on the financial statements of undetected misstatements, if any, could be both material and pervasive the auditor is required to disclaim an opinion.

Equalisation provisions

269. The auditor expresses a qualified opinion if it concludes that the disclosure concerning the equalisation provisions is both inadequate and material to the financial statements. If the auditor concludes that the inadequate disclosure is both material and pervasive to the financial statements the auditor expresses an adverse opinion.

ISA (UK AND IRELAND) 706: EMPHASIS OF MATTER PARAGRAPHS AND OTHER MATTER PARAGRAPHS IN THE INDEPENDENT AUDITOR'S REPORT

Objective

The objective of the auditor, having formed an opinion on the financial statements, is to draw users' attention, when in the auditor's judgment it is necessary to do so, by way of clear additional communication in the auditor's report to:

(a) A matter, although appropriately presented or disclosed in the financial statements, that is of such importance that it is fundamental to users' understanding of the financial statements; or

(b) As appropriate, any other matter that is relevant to users' understanding of the audit, the auditor's responsibilities or the auditor's report. (paragraph 4)

If the auditor considers it necessary to draw users' attention to a matter presented or disclosed in the financial statements that, in the auditor's judgment, is of such importance that it is fundamental to users' understanding of the financial statements, the auditor shall include an Emphasis of Matter paragraph in the auditor's report provided the auditor has obtained sufficient appropriate audit evidence that the matter is not materially misstated in the financial statements. Such a paragraph shall refer only to information presented or disclosed in the financial statements. (paragraph 6)

If the auditor considers it necessary to communicate a matter other than those that are presented or disclosed in the financial statements that, in the auditor's judgment, is relevant to users' understanding of the audit, the auditor's responsibilities or the auditor's report and this is not prohibited by law or regulation, the auditor shall do so in a paragraph in the auditor's report, with the heading "Other Matter" or other appropriate heading. The auditor shall include this paragraph immediately after the Opinion on financial statements paragraph and any Emphasis of Matter paragraph, or elsewhere in the auditor's report if the content of the Other Matter paragraph is relevant to the Other Reporting Responsibilities section. (paragraph 8)

270. Determining technical provisions is subject to a high degree of inherent uncertainty and frequently involves statistical techniques. When reporting on an insurer's financial statements, the auditor evaluates whether such uncertainties fall within the category of significant, and so require to be disclosed in its report. In making this evaluation, the auditor takes into account whether the financial statements provide a user with general information about the types of business written such that the overall level of inherent uncertainty likely to apply to those financial statements is apparent.

271. The fact that an auditor of an insurer has identified that the high estimation uncertainty associated with the calculation of technical provisions gives rise to a significant risk does not automatically require the auditor to include an emphasis of matter paragraph in its auditor's report to draw attention to the financial statement note that describes the uncertainties inherent in the technical provisions.

272. In certain circumstances, the auditor may consider a matter disclosed in the financial statements to be of such importance that it is fundamental to users' understanding of the financial statements that it is appropriate to draw their attention to it. For example, where high estimation uncertainties are in the auditor's opinion a material uncertainty leading to significant doubt about going concern the auditor modifies the auditor's report to include an emphasis of matter paragraph as required by paragraph 19 of ISA (UK and Ireland) 570 and considers whether a duty to report to the regulator exists on which guidance is set out in the section of this Practice Note relating to ISA (UK and Ireland) 250 Section B.

ISA (UK AND IRELAND) 720: SECTION A – THE AUDITOR'S RESPONSIBILITIES RELATING TO OTHER INFORMATION IN DOCUMENTS CONTAINING AUDITED FINANCIAL STATEMENTS

Objective

The objective of the auditor is to respond appropriately when documents containing audited financial statements and the auditor's report thereon include other information that could undermine the credibility of those financial statements and the auditor's report. (paragraph 4)

The auditor shall read the other information to identify material inconsistencies, if any, with the audited financial statements. (paragraph 6)

If, on reading the other information, the auditor identifies a material inconsistency, the auditor shall determine whether the audited financial statements or the other information needs to be revised. (paragraph 8)

If, on reading the other information for the purpose of identifying material inconsistencies, the auditor becomes aware of an apparent material misstatement of fact, the auditor shall discuss the matter with management. (paragraph 14)

273. Insurance companies undertaking long-term business may include supplementary financial statements prepared on an alternative basis to that used in drawing up the financial statements. Without adequate explanation, such supplementary financial statements may appear inconsistent with the audited financial statements. The auditor therefore considers whether an adequate explanation of the assumptions and different methodology has been provided in the annual report, and if not, it considers including an "Other matter" paragraph in its report on the financial statements drawing attention to the inadequacy of the explanation.

274. Supplementary financial statements showing performance arising on long-term business calculated on an alternative basis are prepared using different assumptions and methodologies from those applied in preparing the financial statements. There are many aspects of the supplementary statements not affected by the alternative assumptions and methodologies and where material the auditor considers whether they are treated consistently in both the financial statements and the supplementary financial statements. For those material items where different assumptions and methodologies are applied to the same data to produce the supplementary statements the auditor considers whether consistent data has been used.

275. The auditor reads the supplementary financial statements in the light of knowledge acquired during the audit and considers whether there are any apparent misstatements therein. The auditor is not expected to verify or audit the information contained in the supplementary financial statements.

276. The work of the auditor in reporting to the directors on supplementary financial statements prepared on the alternative method of reporting long term business is outside the scope of this Practice Note.

REPORTING ON REGULATORY RETURNS

277. The auditor of an insurer is required to report on specified matters in relation to returns required from the insurer by its regulator. This section sets out guidance for an auditor reporting on regulatory returns of authorised insurance companies and of Lloyd's syndicates.

The following regulatory returns are covered by this section:

(a) Composite, life and general insurer regulatory returns;

(b) Report on group capital adequacy; and

(c) Lloyd's syndicate Annual Return.

278. An auditor that reports on an insurer's regulatory return often also carries out the audit of its financial statements in accordance with ISAs (UK and Ireland). In such cases, the work that the auditor performs on regulatory returns does not represent a second audit, but represents a set of additional procedures which, in conjunction with the evidence drawn from the audit work carried out in relation to the financial statements, will enable it to report as required. When undertaking such additional procedures the auditor has regard to the Auditors' Code and the general principles set out below.

General Principles
279. The general principles applicable to reporting on regulatory returns are as follows. The auditor:

- Plans the work to be undertaken in relation to the regulatory return so as to perform that work in an effective manner, taking into account its other reporting responsibilities.

- Familiarises itself with the regulations governing the preparation of the regulatory return.

- Complies, where relevant, with APB Ethical Standards for Auditors and with ethical guidance issued by its relevant professional body.

- Agrees the terms of the engagement with the insurer and records them in writing. The auditor may choose to combine the audit requirements in relation to regulatory audits with the financial statement engagement letter, for example in relation to the audit of regulatory returns and the group solvency return (if applicable). In the case of an insurer carrying on long-term insurance business (other than a Lloyd's syndicate), this will include reference to the requirement that the auditor will engage a suitably qualified actuary who is independent of the insurer and pay due regard to advice from that actuary. This actuary is referred to as the Reviewing Actuary[33] by The Institute and Faculty of Actuaries, and this term is used in this section of the Practice Note.

- Considers materiality and its relationship with the risk of material misstatement in the regulatory return in planning its work and in determining the effect of its findings on its report.

- Undertakes its work with an attitude of professional scepticism and performs procedures designed to obtain sufficient appropriate evidence on which to base its opinion on the regulatory return. In particular it:

- Applies analytical procedures in forming an overall conclusion as to whether the regulatory return as a whole is consistent with its knowledge of the insurer's business; and

- Obtains written confirmation of appropriate representations from management before its report is issued.

- Records in its working papers:

  (a) Details of the engagement planning relating to its report on the regulatory return;

  (b) The nature, timing and extent of the procedures performed in relation to its report on the regulatory return, and the conclusions drawn; and

  (c) Its reasoning and conclusions on all significant matters which require the exercise of judgment.

- If reporting on regulatory returns which include financial information on which a component auditor has reported obtain sufficient appropriate evidence that the work of the component auditor is adequate for its purposes.

- Issues a report containing a clear expression of its opinion on the regulatory return.

- Considers the matters which have come to its attention while performing the procedures on the regulatory return and whether they should be included in a report to directors or management.

- Makes a report direct to the FSA and/or Lloyd's if it becomes aware of matters of material significance to the regulator. In addition, when issuing its report on the regulatory return, the auditor:

  (a) Considers whether there are consequential reporting issues affecting its opinion which arise from any report previously made direct to the FSA and/or Lloyd's in the course of the auditor's appointment; and

---

33 Defined in GN 39 and GN 42.

(b) Assesses whether any matters encountered in the course of its work indicate a need for a further direct report.

Authorised insurers

(The following paragraphs do not apply to Lloyd's syndicates, guidance on which is set out in paragraphs 318-328)

280. An insurer regulated by the FSA is required by rule 9.6 of IPRU(INS) to submit a return (the regulatory return) to the FSA within three months of the end of each financial year (reduced to two months and fifteen days if the return is not submitted in an approved electronic form). The format of this return is prescribed by Chapter 9 of IPRU(INS) and its related Appendices. UK incorporated insurers and pure reinsurers (wherever incorporated) are required to prepare a global return covering all business undertaken on a world-wide basis, while direct insurers with head offices outside the EEA are required to prepare both a global return and a UK branch return. Special provisions relate to Swiss direct general insurers and to EEA-deposit insurers.

281. Rule 9.5 of IPRU(INS) requires the regulatory return to be audited in accordance with rule 9.35 by a person qualified in accordance with the rules defined in SUP.

The form and content of the Regulatory Return

282. IPRU(INS) rule 9.3 refers to the central elements of the regulatory return as comprising a revenue account for the year, a balance sheet as at the end of the year and a profit and loss account for the year or, in the case of an insurer not trading for profit, an income and expenditure account for the year. Much of the return is made up of a series of forms designed to provide information of the insurance business undertaken in the form of detailed analyses of a balance sheet and a profit and loss account, as these terms are normally understood, in a format suitable for computer input.

283. The requirement to prepare a regulatory return is quite separate from the requirement for a UK incorporated insurer to prepare financial statements under CA 2006; furthermore, the regulatory return may be prepared some time after the financial statements have been approved. There is, however, a close correlation between the overall figures included in the two documents. Except where over-ridden by the rules in IPRU(INS), words and expressions used in The 2008 Accounts and Reports Regulations have the same meaning within IPRU(INS). In general the rules are drafted so that insurers can apply the same accounting policies in both the regulatory return and the financial statements. In particular GENPRU 1.3 effectively requires that, except where a rule in GENPRU or INSPRU provides for a different method of recognition or valuation, whenever a rule in GENPRU or INSPRU refers to an asset, liability, equity or income statement item, then the insurer for the purposes of that rule, recognises the asset, liability, equity or income statement item and measures it in accordance with UK GAAP or, where EU-IFRSs have been adopted, in accordance with EU-IFRSs.

284. The principal differences between the regulatory return and financial statements prepared under CA 2006 are as follows:

(a) The regulatory return is primarily intended to demonstrate the solvency of an insurer. Copies of the financial statements are also submitted to the regulator;

(b) The balance sheet included in the regulatory return may show items at different values from those shown in the financial statements, arising from the application of prescribed rules in respect of: –

   (i) The assets that can be treated as admissible; assets that are not admissible (for example deferred acquisition costs in respect of long-term business) are left out of account;

   (ii) The basic valuation principles to be applied to admissible assets and to liabilities; – restrictions on the value of assets where the value arrived at by applying the basic valuation principles exceeds the permitted market risk or counterparty exposure limits; and

   (iii) The determination of long-term insurance business liabilities; – the treatment of certain types of hybrid capital; and – a provision for reasonable foreseeable adverse variations where certain commitments are not strictly matched;

(c) The income statement, particularly for general business, provides a large volume of detailed segmental information including a breakdown into combined categories and further sub-divisions into material risk categories, which are reported by currency and, in some cases, reporting territory. Deposit accounting must not be used in the income statement for long-term insurance contracts even where these contracts are subject to deposit accounting as investment business in the financial statements;

(d) Additional information is provided on a variety of topics including:

   • The Abstract of the valuation, prepared by the actuarial function holder(s) for an insurer carrying on long-term insurance business.

   • General business reinsurance arrangements.

   • Financial reinsurance and other financing arrangements.

   • Major general business reinsurers and cedants.

   • The use of derivatives.

   • Controllers.

   • The interests of the actuary appointed to perform the with-profits actuary function; and

(e) The regulatory return is accompanied by a certificate signed by prescribed officers of the insurer ("the certificate") which contains a number of statements including a statement that the return has been properly prepared in accordance with the requirements in IPRU(INS), INSPRU and GENPRU. The certificate is outside the scope of the audit.

The auditor's responsibilities

285. Part II of Appendix 9.6 to IPRU(INS) indicates the matters that must be included in the auditor's report. The basic elements prescribed are:

(a) Whether in the auditor's opinion:

  (i) The documents referred to in rules 9.12, 9.13 and 9.14, together with Forms 40 to 45, 48, 49, 56, 58 and 60 and the statements, analyses and reports annexed pursuant to rules 9.24 to 9.27, 9.29 and 9.31 of IPRU(INS) have been properly prepared in accordance with the Accounts and Statements Rules, GENPRU and INSPRU[34]; and

  (ii) The methods and assumptions determined by the insurer and used to perform the actuarial investigation (as set out in the valuation reports) appropriately reflect the requirements of INSPRU 1.2 and INSPRU 1.3; and

(b) That, in accordance with rule 9.35(1A), to the extent that any document, Form, statement, analysis or report to be audited under rule 9.35(1) contains amounts or information abstracted from the actuarial investigation performed pursuant to rule 9.4, the auditor has obtained and paid due regard to advice from a suitably qualified actuary who is independent of the insurer.

286. In addition, IPRU(INS) 9.35(2)[35] requires the auditor to report by exception if it is of the opinion that:

(a) Adequate accounting records have not been kept, or that returns adequate for its audit have not been received from branches not visited by it;

(b) The insurer's individual accounts are not in agreement with the accounting records and returns; and

(c) It has failed to obtain all the information and explanations which, to the best of the auditor's knowledge and belief, are necessary for the purposes of the audit.

---

34 The illustrative example regulatory reports in Appendices 1.2 to 1.4 set out the specific Forms and statements that are reported on by the auditor.
35 IPRU INS 9.35(2) achieves this by applying sections 498(1), (2) and (3) of CA 2006. It also applies section 498(1) of CA 2006 which addresses the auditor's general right to information.

Standards to be applied by the auditor

287. In the case of a UK incorporated insurer, an audit of the financial statements prepared under CA 2006 will be conducted in accordance with ISAs (UK and Ireland) issued by the APB to enable the report required by section 495 of CA 2006 to be given. Key areas in which the auditor needs to undertake procedures additional to those undertaken to report on the financial statements are:

   (a) The application of the prescribed valuation and admissibility rules to assets and liabilities for which existence, title, etc. has already been considered as a part of the audit of the insurer's financial statements;

   (b) The sub-division of general business revenue information into the prescribed categories;

   (c) Presentation of the information in the prescribed forms; and

   (d) The specific additional disclosures that fall within the scope of the auditor's report.

288. If an audit of financial statements in accordance with ISAs (UK and Ireland) has not been undertaken (as may be the case in relation to the UK branch of an insurer incorporated outside the UK) the regulatory return will need to have been subjected to an audit in accordance with those Standards in order to achieve an equivalent standard of evidence.

289. Work specific to the auditor's report on an insurer's regulatory return may be undertaken concurrently with procedures designed to provide evidence for its report on the financial statements or at a later date. In either case, the auditor considers both aspects of the engagement when planning the audit of the financial statements.

290. Although IPRU(INS) does not require the regulatory return to be drawn up to show a true and fair view, rule 9.11 of IPRU(INS) requires that the return:

   "must fairly state the information provided on the basis required by the Accounts and Statements Rules".

291. This is of a similar qualitative standard to the requirement of company law that financial statements prepared in accordance with UK GAAP give a true and fair view of a company's state of affairs and profit or loss, hence equivalent considerations of materiality apply. In evaluating whether the requirements of rule 9.11 have been met, the auditor therefore applies materiality in relation to the business as a whole, rather than in relation to the particular business reporting category within which a particular item is reported. Following this approach, reliance on analytical review techniques may be appropriate in relation to, for example, the segmental information provided within the regulatory return.

The Auditor's Procedures on Regulatory Returns Long-term business

292. The auditor's reporting responsibilities are set out in paragraph 285 above.

293. As also noted above, rule 9.35(1A) of IPRU(INS) requires that where any part of the regulatory return that is subject to audit contains amounts or information abstracted from the actuarial investigation, the auditor is required to obtain and pay due regard to advice from a Reviewing Actuary who is independent of the insurer and suitably qualified.

294. The actuarial investigation includes:

"(a) A determination of the liabilities of the insurer attributable to its long-term insurance business;

(b) A valuation of any excess over those liabilities of the assets representing the long-term insurance fund or funds and, where any rights of any long-term policy holders to participate in profits relate to particular parts of such a fund a valuation of any excess of assets over liabilities in respect of each of those parts; and

(c) For every long-term insurer which is a realistic basis life firm, a calculation of the with profits insurance capital component."

295. The FSA Handbook does not set out the nature of the advice to be obtained from the Reviewing Actuary or provide guidance on the nature or extent of the work to be performed by the Reviewing Actuary in providing that advice. The responsibility for determining the nature of the advice and, consequently, the scope and extent of the Reviewing Actuary's work lies with the auditor, although the auditor discusses the proposed scope of work with the Reviewing Actuary and considers the views of the Reviewing Actuary before finalising the scope of work.

296. The auditor obtains advice from the Reviewing Actuary on those elements of the actuarial investigation that the auditor believes, for the purpose of the audit of the annual return, require expert actuarial input to assess. The areas of the actuarial investigation that the auditor will seek advice from a Reviewing Actuary on include whether:

- The methods and assumptions used to calculate the mathematical reserves appropriately reflect the requirements of INSPRU 1.2 ("Mathematical reserves").

- The methods and assumptions used to calculate the "With-profits insurance capital component ("WPICC") appropriately reflect the requirements of INSPRU 1.3 ("With-profits insurance capital component").

- The statement(s) made under rule 9.31 of IPRU(INS) ("Valuation reports on long-term insurance business") are made in accordance with the requirements of Appendix 9.4 and Appendix 9.4A of IPRU(INS).

297. In addition to obtaining advice on the matters set out in the preceding paragraph, the auditor obtains advice on all other elements of the actuarial investigation to the extent that they are relevant to the auditable parts of the return. The elements of the actuarial investigation, other than those detailed above, that the auditor may also seek to obtain advice from the Reviewing Actuary on include whether:

- The data underlying the calculation of the mathematical reserves and WPICC are reliable.

- The models used to apply the methods and assumptions underlying the mathematical reserves and WPICC are operating appropriate.

- The data contained in Forms 18, 19, 48, 49, 56, 58 and 60 have been correctly abstracted from the actuarial valuation.

- The data contained in lines 51 and 52 of Form 11 have been correctly abstracted from the actuarial valuation (for insurers which transact health insurance).

Consideration of the guidance as set out above, is likely to be of particular relevance to the auditor where the auditable parts of the return include disclosure of data at the level of type of product or class of contract. Disclosures in this level of detail are included in the Valuation Reports required under rule 9.31 of IPRU(INS).

298. The auditor engages the Reviewing Actuary to perform work to the scope the auditor, following discussion with the Reviewing Actuary, determines is appropriate. Whilst the formality of these arrangements may vary depending on whether the Reviewing Actuary is with a third party firm of actuaries or is an employee or partner of the auditor or its member firms, the auditor will agree in writing the scope of work and reporting by the Reviewing Actuary. It is expected that this will include, among other things,

- The scope of work to be performed by the Reviewing Actuary including the areas of the actuarial investigation and auditable parts of the return on which the Reviewing Actuary will perform work and details of the nature and scope of the work to be performed.

- The form of the review that the auditor will carry out on the work of the Reviewing Actuary.

- The form of report to be issued to the auditor containing the advice from the Reviewing Actuary.

- A requirement that the Reviewing Actuary will perform its work having due regard to relevant guidance issued by The Faculty and Institute of Actuaries and the Technical Actuarial Standards (TASs) issued by BAS and will notify the auditor immediately it becomes aware of any matters that may indicate non-compliance with the guidance.

- Protocols for the timely reporting to the auditor of any issues arising in relation to the duty to report matters of material significance to the FSA.

- Arrangements for the confirmation of the Reviewing Actuary's independence and qualifications (if not an employee or partner of the auditor or its member firms).

- A requirement for the Reviewing Actuary to notify the auditor immediately of any significant facts and matters that bear upon the Reviewing Actuary's objectivity and independence.

Establishing the independence of the Reviewing Actuary

299. The auditor should be satisfied that any Reviewing Actuary will be independent and document the rationale for that conclusion. Guidance for the auditor on establishing the independence of the Reviewing Actuary is set out below.

300. When planning the audit of the regulatory return, the engagement partner obtains information from the Reviewing Actuary as to the existence of any connections that the Reviewing Actuary has with the client including:

- Financial interests.
- Business relationships (including the provision of services).
- Employment (past, present and future).
- Family and other personal relationships.

301. The engagement partner assesses the threats to objectivity and independence that arise from any connections disclosed and considers whether the Reviewing Actuary has implemented safeguards to eliminate the threats or reduce them to an acceptable level.

302. When assessing the threats to objectivity and independence which arise from services provided to the client or its affiliates and the effectiveness of safeguards established by the actuarial firm, the engagement partner will consider the following factors:

   (a) Whether the Reviewing Actuary was the person responsible for the service provided;

   (b) The materiality and the nature of the services to the actuarial firm; and

   (c) The extent to which the outcomes of services have been reviewed by another actuarial firm.

303. In certain circumstances, it is unlikely that any safeguards can eliminate the threat to objectivity and independence or reduce it to an acceptable level. Such circumstances are likely to include:

- Direct financial interests in the client or an affiliate held by the actuarial firm, the Reviewing Actuary, any member of the Reviewing Actuary's team, or immediate family members of such persons.

- Material business relationships with the client or an affiliate entered into by the actuarial firm, the Reviewing Actuary, any member of the Reviewing Actuary's team, or immediate family members of such persons.

- Any connection that enables the client to influence the affairs of the actuarial firm, or the performance of any actuarial review engagement undertaken by the firm.

- Situations involving any employment[36] of the Reviewing Actuary or any member of the Reviewing Actuary's team, in the past two years, or their current or potential employment with the client.

- Situations involving employment of immediate family members of the Reviewing Actuary, or any member of the Reviewing Actuary's team by the client in a key management position.

- In the case of listed companies, where the Reviewing Actuary has acted in this role for a continuous period longer than seven years.

- Situations where more than 10% of the total fees of the actuarial firm are regularly receivable from the client and its subsidiaries.

- Any contingent fee arrangements for services provided to the client and its affiliates by the actuarial firm where the fee is dependent on a future or contemporary actuarial judgment.

- Any engagement in the current period of the actuarial firm to provide actuarial valuation or financial reporting services to the client[37] or services where the objectives of the engagement are inconsistent with the objectives of the work of the Reviewing Actuary.

304. The engagement partner requires the Reviewing Actuary to notify him or her immediately of changes in the circumstances on which information was obtained at the start of the engagement, or any others that might reasonably be considered a threat to the Reviewing Actuaries objectivity.

305. Where the engagement partner identifies a significant threat to objectivity and independence which has not been eliminated or reduced to an acceptable level, he/she discusses with the FSA the circumstances that give rise to the threat and what course of

---

36 Employment includes appointment to the board of directors of the audit client, any sub-committee of the board, or to such a position in an entity that holds, directly or indirectly, more than 20% of the voting rights in the audit client, or in which the audit client holds directly or indirectly more than 20% of the voting rights.

37 This will include a service to act as Actuarial Function Holder or a With-profits Actuary.

action would be appropriate, including obtaining a rule waiver from the FSA. In circumstances where the matter cannot be resolved satisfactorily, the engagement partner considers making a reference to the independence of the Reviewing Actuary in the report made to the FSA.

Reviewing the work of the Reviewing Actuary

306. When obtaining and paying due regard to the advice of a Reviewing Actuary the auditor has regard to ISA (UK and Ireland) 620. In accordance with paragraph A13 of ISA (UK and Ireland) 620, when the auditor uses the work of an internal expert the auditor is entitled to rely on the firm's system of quality control, unless information provided by the firm or other parties indicates otherwise as explained in paragraph 4 of ISA (UK and Ireland) 220.

307. As required by ISA (UK and Ireland) 620 the auditor evaluates the adequacy of the Reviewing Actuary's work for the auditor's purposes with respect to the annual return being considered. This involves evaluating:

- The relevance and reasonableness of the Reviewing Actuaries findings or conclusions, and their consistency with other evidence.
- The relevance, completeness and accuracy of the source data used.
- The relevance and reasonableness of the assumptions and methods used.
- When the Reviewing Actuary carried out the work.
- The reasons for any changes in assumptions and methods compared with those used in the prior period.

308. When considering whether the Reviewing Actuary has used source data which is significant to the actuaries work and relevant in the circumstances, the auditor may consider performing the following procedures:

  (a) Making enquiries regarding any procedures undertaken by the Reviewing Actuary to establish whether the source data is relevant, complete, accurate and internally consistent;

  (b) Verifying the origin of the data, including obtaining an understanding of, and where applicable testing, the internal controls over the data and, where relevant its transmission to the expert;

  and

  (c) Reviewing or testing the data used by the Reviewing Actuary.

309. The auditor does not have the same expertise as the Reviewing Actuary; however, it seeks to obtain an understanding of the assumptions and methods used by the insurer

and to consider whether they are reasonable, based on the auditor's knowledge of the business. If the results of the Reviewing Actuary's work are not consistent with other audit evidence, the auditor attempts to resolve the inconsistency by discussions with the Reviewing Actuary. Applying additional procedures, including possibly engaging another Reviewing Actuary, may also assist in resolving the inconsistency. If the auditor is not satisfied that the work of the Reviewing Actuary provides sufficient appropriate audit evidence to support its opinion on the regulatory returns and there is no satisfactory alternative source of audit evidence, the auditor considers the implications for its auditor's report.

Reporting

310. Auditor's reports on regulatory returns normally include the following matters:

   (a) A title identifying the persons to whom the report is addressed (which will normally be the directors of the insurer);

   (b) An introductory paragraph identifying the documents within the regulatory return which are covered by the report;

   (c) Separate sections, appropriately headed, dealing with:

      (i)   Respective responsibilities of the insurer and the auditor, and

      (ii) The basis of the auditor's opinion;

   (d) The auditor's opinions on the matters required by the rules;

   (e) The signature of the auditor; and

   (f) The date of the auditor's report.

   If the FSA has issued any directions to the insurer, waiving or modifying the application of any rules that affect the audited parts of a regulatory return, the auditor refers to these in the report and expresses the opinions by reference to the rules as modified.

311. Examples 1.1 to 1.3 of Appendix 1 set out illustrative examples of reports on regulatory returns for composite, life and general insurers. These illustrative examples need to be tailored to reflect particular circumstances.

312. Rule 9.3 of IPRU(INS) requires every insurer to prepare with respect to each financial year a revenue account, a balance sheet and a profit and loss account. While the global regulatory return might be regarded as the responsibility of the board of directors in the same way as for financial statements, in the case of a UK branch regulatory return, it is required to be signed by the principal UK Executive and the UK Authorised Representative. Consequently, the illustrative reports set out in the appendices refer to "the insurer" rather than "the directors", when referring to the respective responsibilities.

Subsequent events

313. There may be a gap between the date on which an insurer's statutory financial statements are approved and the date on which it's regulatory return is signed. The auditor undertakes a review of post-balance sheet events up to the date of its report on the regulatory return before signing that report.

Modifying the auditor's opinion

314. When reporting on an insurer's regulatory returns, the auditor modifies its opinion as appropriate, following the principles in ISA (UK and Ireland) 705. It is possible for the auditor's opinion on an insurer's financial statements to be modified whilst that on its regulatory return is unmodified, and vice versa. This may occur where the grounds for modification relate to the treatment of a particular item (for example, if an asset is included in the regulatory return at a value which does not take account of the specific requirements of the rules relating to the valuation or admissibility of assets). Any modification in respect of technical provisions would (in the absence of exceptional circumstances such as a Court judgment clarifying liability after the signing of the financial statements) be expected to be reflected in both opinions.

315. When the auditor modifies its report, on the regulatory return, by making reference to an uncertainty, Appendix 9.6 of IPRU(INS) requires the auditor to state whether, in its opinion, the uncertainty is material to determining whether the insurer has available assets in excess of its capital resources requirement.

316. Included in the regulatory return is a description of the insurance business undertaken by the insurer which is outside the scope of the audit and as such the auditor is not required to express an opinion on this statement. Therefore, despite the general requirement in ISA (UK and Ireland) 720 Section A, the auditor need not read the certificate to identify any inconsistencies with the audited elements of the return. If, however, the auditor becomes aware of any apparent misstatements in the certificate or identifies any material inconsistencies with the audited elements of the return, the auditor seeks to resolve them. This principle should be extended to include any other form, statement, analysis or report required to be included in the return but not subject to audit.

Resubmitted returns

317. The FSA may require the insurer to resubmit the regulatory return, or part thereof, where the original regulatory return is considered to be inaccurate or incomplete. The auditor is normally required to express an opinion on the amended or additional material. This can be done by either:

    (a) Withdrawing the original report and issuing a completely new report under rule 9.35 of IPRU(INS); or

(b) Issuing a supplementary report on the amended material only, but including a reference to the original report.

The first option is preferable where the nature and volume of changes required gives rise to a resubmission of the complete return. The second option is preferable where the amendments are considered to be relatively minor or are few in number and only the amended forms, supplementary notes and/or statements are resubmitted.

Lloyd's syndicates

318. The purpose of the syndicate Annual Return is:

(a) To assist Lloyd's in preparing the market aggregate accounts in accordance with the 2008 Regulations and preparing the regulatory return to the FSA giving an overall view of solvency and performance of the market;

(b) To make solvency test adjustments to reflect the application of prescribed assets and liabilities valuation rules as follows:

- The basic valuation principles to be applied to admissible assets;

- Restrictions on the value of assets where the value arrived at by applying the basic valuation principles exceeds the permitted asset exposure limits;

- The basic valuation principles to be applied to the determination of liabilities for solvency test purposes in respect of each year of account included in the syndicate Annual Return; and

(c) To disclose such additional information as is specified by Lloyd's.

The syndicate Annual Return includes a managing agent's report to be attached to each submission signed by officers of the agency. The scope of these reports is prescribed by Lloyd's. There are no separate requirements for audited regulatory reports in respect of Lloyd's corporate members.

Auditor's responsibilities

319. Certain of the submissions of the syndicate Annual Return require an auditor's report to be included. The scope of these reports is prescribed by Lloyd's.

Standards to be applied by auditors

320. In the case of a Lloyd's syndicate, the audit of its annual accounts and, where appropriate, underwriting year accounts conducted in accordance with ISAs (UK and Ireland) underlie the relevant reports to be made. Key areas in which the auditor needs to undertake procedures in relation to the syndicate Annual Return additional to those undertaken to report on the financial statements include:

- The application of the prescribed valuation and admissibility rules to assets and liabilities for which existence, title, etc. should have already been considered as a part of the audit of the syndicate's financial statements.

- The prescribed analysis of accounting information.

- Presentation of the information in the prescribed form.

- The systems and procedures operated by the managing agent.

- Any specific additional disclosures that fall within the scope of the auditor's report.

321. The auditor may report on parts of the syndicate Annual Return before reporting on the annual accounts and underwriting year accounts. If all aspects of audit work on these accounts are not yet complete, it will need to be satisfied that any matters outstanding with respect to that work will be unlikely to result in changes to the information contained in the relevant part of the syndicate Annual Return. This means that the audit of these accounts must be at an advanced stage and that, subject only to unforeseen events, the auditor expects to be in a position to issue its report on these accounts incorporating the information contained in the return, and know what that report will say. This means completing the audit, including any appropriate reviews by personnel not otherwise involved in the audit as described in ISA (UK and Ireland) 220, subject only to the following:

(a) Clearing outstanding audit matters which the auditor is satisfied are unlikely to have a material impact on the annual accounts and underwriting year accounts;

(b) Completing audit procedures on the detail of note disclosures to the annual accounts and underwriting year accounts that will not have a material impact on those accounts;

(c) Updating the subsequent events review to cover the period between reporting on the syndicate Annual Return and reporting on those accounts (if appropriate); and

(d) Obtaining written representations, where relevant, from management and establishing that those accounts have been approved by the directors of the managing agent.

322. Lloyd's prescribes from time to time the information to be reported in the syndicate Annual Return, how that information is to be reported (e.g. format and content of the return and the allocation of information across the various submissions) the scope of agents', actuaries' and auditor's reports, and the timetable for making the various submissions and annexed reports. The syndicate auditor will need to familiarise itself with such requirements as they are prescribed and to consider their impact on its

work. In particular, changes by Lloyd's over time to the prescribed scope of its report, or reports, may indicate that changes (including deletions, additions and amendments) are needed to the syndicate auditor's work programme in order to support the revised opinions.

323. The syndicate Annual Return may be required to report information at a level of detail which goes beyond the level of disclosure in syndicate annual accounts or underwriting accounts. Having regard to the prescribed scope of the auditor's report on the syndicate Annual Return, or different reports on separate submissions thereof, the auditor applies materiality in relation to the business as a whole, rather than in relation to the particular detailed analysis within which a particular item is reported. Following this approach, reliance on analytical review techniques may be appropriate in relation to, for example, the segmental and other detailed information within the syndicate Annual Return.

The Auditor's Procedures on Regulatory Returns

324. The FSA has sole responsibility for the regulation and supervision of the Lloyd's market in line with the regulation and supervision of other UK insurers. Lloyd's imposes its own regulations and requirements on the market to enable it to comply with its own reporting obligations to the FSA and overseas regulators and to regulate its own rules. The Society and Lloyd's underwriting agents are subject to regulation by the FSA. At the present time, members of Lloyd's are not regulated directly by the FSA although FSMA 2000 enables the FSA to do so.

325. Lloyd's is required to file a full scope regulatory return with the FSA for the market as a whole which incorporates a demonstration that each member has sufficient assets to meet its underwriting liabilities. The overall return is reported on by the syndicate auditor to the Society of Lloyd's in terms specified in the FSA Handbook. The auditor is aware that information contained in returns on which the syndicate auditor has issued a report will be included in the market-level regulatory return to the FSA.

Modifying the auditor's report

326. When reporting on submissions of syndicate Annual Returns, the auditor includes an emphasis of matter or qualifies its opinion as appropriate following the principles in ISAs (UK and Ireland) 705 and 706. It is possible for the auditor's opinion in its report on a syndicate Annual Return submission to be qualified whilst that on the annual accounts or underwriting accounts is unqualified and vice versa. This may occur where the grounds for qualification relate to the treatment of a particular item (for example, if an asset or a liability is included in the syndicate Annual Return at a value which does not take account of the specific requirements of the Lloyd's Valuation of Liabilities Rules or the Eligible Asset Rules). Any qualification or emphasis of matter paragraph in respect of technical provisions would normally be expected to be reflected in both reports.

Resubmitted returns

327. As stated above Lloyd's may require the syndicate to resubmit the syndicate Annual Return, or part thereof, where the original return is not considered to meet Lloyd's criteria; the auditor may be required to express an opinion on the amended or additional material. This can be done by either:

(a) Withdrawing the original report and issuing a new report; or

(b) Issuing a supplementary report on the amended material only, but including reference to the original report.

328. The first option is preferable where the nature and volume of changes required gives rise to a resubmission of the complete return. The second option is preferable where the amendments are considered to be relatively minor or are few in number and only the amended pages of the return are resubmitted.

Auditor's statements on Group Capital Adequacy

329. The EU Insurance Groups Directive requires regulators not only to monitor insurance companies for which they have regulatory responsibility but also to monitor the solvency of insurance groups to which those firms belong. As a consequence rule 9.40(1) of IPRU(INS) requires an insurer to which INSPRU 6.1 applies to provide to the FSA in respect of its ultimate insurance parent undertaking and its ultimate EEA insurance parent undertaking (if different), a report of:

(a) The group capital resources of that undertaking (as calculated in accordance with INSPRU 6.1.36R);

(b) The group capital resources requirement of that undertaking (as calculated in accordance with INSPRU 6.1.33R); and

(c) Subject to certain exceptions, particulars of any member of the insurance group which is in a position of regulatory solvency deficit.

Where more than one insurer have a common insurance parent undertaking, one of the insurers may submit the report on behalf of all the insurers in the insurance group.

330. An insurer is not required to submit the report where it is a non-EEA insurer or where under Article 4(2) of the Insurance Groups Directive, the competent authority of an EEA State other than the United Kingdom has agreed to be the competent authority responsible for exercising supplementary supervision.

331. The report required in respect of insurance group capital adequacy must include a statement from the auditor of the insurer that, in its opinion, the report has been properly

compiled in accordance with INSPRU 6.1 and rule 9.40(1) of IPRU (INS) from information provided by members of the insurance group and from the insurer's own records.

332. The information and calculations to be provided by an insurer under rule 9.40(1) of IPRU(INS) is in respect of the insurer and each member of its insurance group[38]. The insurance group consists of the insurer's ultimate insurance parent undertaking and its related undertakings or where the parent is itself an insurer (a participating insurance undertaking) the insurer and its related undertakings. An insurance parent undertaking is:

   (a) A participating insurance undertaking which has a subsidiary undertaking that is an insurance undertaking; or

   (b) An insurance holding company which has a subsidiary undertaking which is an insurer; or

   (c) An insurance undertaking (not within (a)) which has a subsidiary undertaking which is an insurer.

333. The auditor's report under 9.40(3)(c) of IPRU(INS) requires the auditor to state that, in its opinion, the report has been properly compiled in accordance with INSPRU 6.1 from information provided by members of the insurance group and from the insurer's own records. The auditor is not required to perform any independent examination of the underlying financial information upon which the information in the submission to the FSA is based.

334. To make the statement required by rule 9.40(3)(c) of IPRU(INS) the auditor will normally:

   (a) Read any instructions issued to other members of the insurance group and compare these with the requirements set out in INSPRU 6.1;

   (b) Compare on a test basis, the information provided to the insurer by other members of the insurance group and any adjustments made by the insurer thereto, with

      (i)   The instructions (if any) issued by the insurer,

      (ii) The basis upon which the information has been produced,

      (iii) The requirements set out in INSPRU 6.1;

   (c) Compare, on a test basis, the compilation of the Report with the information provided to the insurer by other members of the insurance group and with information from the insurer's own records;

---

38 If the parent is not only a participating insurance undertaking but an insurer with its head office in the UK, its insurance subsidiaries are not required to submit the report, although some ancillary reporting may be required.

(d) Confirm the mathematical accuracy of the compilation of the financial information contained in the Report; and

(e) Identify any significant areas where the information included in the submission may not comply with the above.

An example auditor's statement in respect of group capital adequacy is set out as example 1.4 of Appendix 1.

335. The additional information on group capital adequacy required to be reported to the FSA under rule 9.40(1A) of IPRU(INS) is not within the scope of the auditor's statement on group capital adequacy. Therefore, the group capital adequacy report is structured so that the auditor's statement clearly identifies those parts of the group capital adequacy report within the scope of the auditor's statement.

336. Rule 9.42A of IPRU(INS) requires that insurers make available to the public certain specified information on the group capital adequacy position but do not require the auditor to report on this publicly available information.

337. An insurer may be a member of a financial conglomerate and as such may be required to submit a return that is analogous to the group capital adequacy report for an insurance group. Where the financial conglomerate is an insurance conglomerate (other than one to which SUP 16.12.32R(1)(a) applies) SUP 16.12.33R requires the auditor to provide a statement on this return in accordance with rule 9.40(3)(c) of IPRU(INS). The auditor will follow the guidance in this section of this Practice Note, with suitable amendments (e.g. to make reference to the relevant rules in SUP in addition to those in IPRU(INS)).

Auditor's review reports on interim net profits

338. An insurer must maintain at all times capital resources equal to or in excess of its capital resources requirement. In the case of a composite insurer this requirement applies separately to capital resources in respect of both its long-term insurance business and general insurance business. An insurer may include interim net profits in its capital resources (calculated in accordance with Stage A of the calculation in the Capital Resources Table in GENPRU 2 Annex 1R) only if those interim net profits have been externally verified by an insurer's auditor. The auditor may, for this reason, be asked to report on the interim net profits of an insurer, for capital adequacy purposes.

339. Interim net profits in this context means, net profits of the insurer as at a date specified by the insurer after the end of its most recently audited financial year end and up to and including its next financial year end, calculated after deductions for tax, declared dividends and other appropriations.

340. GENPRU 2.2.102R does not include specific guidance as to what constitutes an external verification. However "verification" as used in the context of GENPRU is understood to

indicate a degree of assurance which is lower than that given by a full audit. An engagement to "verify" interim profits may therefore be taken to be a review engagement, and an opinion may be given in terms of negative assurance. The report is normally addressed to the directors of the insurer.

341. As an external "verification" of interim net profits does not require a full scope audit it will be important for the FSA, in considering the adequacy of the "verification" of interim profits, to be informed of the procedures that have been undertaken by the auditor, in support of its opinion. This is particularly important in the case of insurers where no prescribed procedures have been established by the FSA themselves in rules or guidance. Consequently the detailed scope of the work undertaken by the auditor in support of its opinion is listed in the auditor's report or included in the report by reference to the letter of engagement where the programme of work has been laid down.

342. In undertaking the review the auditor normally performs the following procedures:

(a) Satisfies itself that the figures forming the basis of the interim net profits have been properly extracted from the underlying accounting records;

(b) Reviews the accounting policies used in calculating the interim net profits for the period under review so as to obtain comfort that they are consistent with those normally adopted by the insurer in drawing up its annual financial statements and, as applicable, are in accordance with , EU-IFRSs, UK GAAP and the Insurance SORP as applicable;

(c) Performs analytical procedures on the results to date which form the basis of calculating the interim net profits, including comparisons of the actual performance to date with budget and with the results of the prior period(s);

(d) Discusses with management the overall performance and financial position of the insurer;

(e) Obtains adequate comfort that the implications of current and prospective litigation (not in the ordinary course of insurance business), all known contingencies and commitments, changes in business activities and the determination of insurance technical provisions have been properly taken into account in arriving at the interim net profits; and

(f) Follows up significant matters of which the auditor is already aware in the course of auditing the insurer's most recent financial statements.

The auditor may also consider obtaining appropriate representations from management.

343. The auditor makes it clear that the report has been produced for the use of the insurer in meeting the requirements of the FSA for the purposes of the calculation of its capital resources only. This may be clarified in the report and/or in the engagement letter. An illustrative report is included as example 1.6 of Appendix 1.

APPENDIX 1

ILLUSTRATIVE EXAMPLES OF AUDITOR'S REPORTS

The APB publishes, periodically, a "Compendium of Illustrative Auditor's Report's on United Kingdom Private Sector Financial Statements" in the form of a Bulletin. At the time of publication of this Practice Note the latest Compendium Bulletin was 2010/2 which includes the following illustrative examples relating to insurers:

- Example 17: Publicly traded insurer with a standard listing preparing financial statements under UK GAAP and having equalisation provisions

- Example 18: Lloyd's syndicate – annual financial statements
- Example 19: Lloyd's syndicate – underwriting year accounts – closed year of account
- Example 20: Lloyd's syndicate – underwriting year accounts – run-off year of account

This appendix contains the following example auditor's reports:

Reports on regulatory returns

1.1   Composite insurer

1.2   Life insurer

1.3   General insurer

1.4   Statement on the group capital adequacy report

Reports relating to a Lloyd's syndicate

1.5   Personal and syndicate MAPA accounts

Other reports by the auditor

1.6   Report on interim net profits

When reporting on an insurer's regulatory return, the example reports set out in this Appendix need to be adapted to meet the circumstances of that insurer, taking account of the notes set out in the Appendix.

In the case of a partial resubmission, the reports will indicate that the documents being reported upon have been prepared as amended documents to replace the corresponding documents on which the auditor reported on [....... XX].

1.1 – REGULATORY REPORT: COMPOSITE INSURER

.........................[COMPOSITE INSURANCE COMPANY LIMITED]

[Global business/UK branch business]

Financial year ended 31 December 201x

Independent auditor's report to the directors pursuant to rule 9.35 of the Interim Prudential Sourcebook for Insurers ("IPRU(INS)")
We have audited the following documents prepared by the insurer pursuant to the Accounts and Statements Rules set out in Part I and Part IV of Chapter 9 to IPRU(INS) the Interim Prudential Sourcebook for Insurers, GENPRU the General Prudential Sourcebook and INSPRU the Prudential Sourcebook for Insurers ("the Rules") made by the Financial Services Authority under section 138 of the Financial Services and Markets Act 2000:

- Forms **[1 to 3, 10 to 32, 34, 36 to 45, 48, 49, 56, 58 and 60]**, (including the supplementary notes) on pages [...] to [...] ("the Forms");

- the statements required by IPRU(INS) rules 9.25, 9.26, 9.27 and 9.29 on pages [...] to [...] ("the statements"); and

- the valuation report[s] required by IPRU(INS) rule 9.31[(a)] on pages [...] to [...] (the valuation report[s]).

We are not required to audit and do not express an opinion on:

- Forms **[46, 47, 50 to 55, 57, 59A and 59B]** (including the supplementary notes) on pages [...] to [...];

- the statements required by IPRU(INS) rules 9.30, 9.32, 9.32A and 9.36[39] on pages [...] to [...]; and

- the certificate required by IPRU(INS) rule 9.34(1) on pages [...] to [...] .

Respective responsibilities of the insurer and its auditor
The insurer is responsible for the preparation of an annual return (including the Forms, the statements and the valuation report[s]) under the provisions of the Rules. **[The requirements of the Rules have been modified by [a] direction[s] issued under section 148 of the Financial Services and Markets Act 2000 on ....200X [and ....200X]**. Under IPRU(INS) rule 9.11 the Forms, the statements, and the valuation report[s] are required to be prepared in the manner specified by the Rules and to state fairly the information provided on the basis required by the Rules. The methods and assumptions determined by the insurer and

---

39   Required where there is a With-Profits Actuary.

used to perform the actuarial investigation as set out in the valuation report[s] are required to reflect appropriately the requirements of INSPRU 1.2 [and 1.3[40]].

It is our responsibility to form an independent opinion as to whether the Forms, the statements, the valuation report[s] meet these requirements, and to report our opinion to you. We also report to you if, in our opinion:

- adequate accounting records have not been kept, or returns adequate for our audit have not been received from branches not visited by us; or

- the Forms, the statements and the valuation report[s] are not in agreement with the accounting records and returns; or

- we have not received all the information we require for our audit.

Basis of opinion
We conducted our work in accordance with Practice Note 20 "The audit of insurers in the United Kingdom (Revised)" issued by the Auditing Practices Board. Our work included examination, on a test basis, of evidence relevant to the amounts and disclosures in the Forms, the statements and the valuation report[s]. The evidence included that previously obtained by us relating to the audit of the financial statements of the insurer for the financial year. It also included an assessment of the significant estimates and judgments made by the insurer in the preparation of the Forms, the statements and the valuation report[s].

We planned and performed our work so as to obtain all the information and explanations which we considered necessary in order to provide us with sufficient evidence to give reasonable assurance that the Forms, the statements and the valuation report[s] are free from material misstatement, whether caused by fraud or other irregularity or error and comply with IPRU(INS) rule 9.11.

In accordance with IPRU(INS) rule 9.35(1A), to the extent that any document, Form, statement, analysis or report to be examined under IPRU(INS) rule 9.35(1) contains amounts or information abstracted from the actuarial investigation performed pursuant to IPRU(INS) rule 9.4, we have obtained and paid due regard to advice from a suitably qualified actuary who is independent of the insurer.

Opinion
In our opinion:

(i) the Forms, the statements and the valuation report[s] fairly state the information provided on the basis required by the Rules [as modified] and have been properly prepared in accordance with the provisions of those Rules; and

---

40 Required for "Realistic Basis" firms only.

(ii) the methods and assumptions determined by the insurer and used to perform the actuarial investigation as set out in the valuation report[s] appropriately reflect the requirements of INSPRU 1.2 (and 1.3).

Statutory auditor   *Address*
Date

1.2 – REGULATORY REPORT: LIFE INSURER

.... [LIFE INSURANCE COMPANY LIMITED]

[Global business/UK branch business]

Financial year ended 31 December 201x

Independent auditor's report to the directors pursuant to rule 9.35 of the Interim Prudential Sourcebook for Insurers ("IPRU(INS)")

We have audited the following documents prepared by the insurer pursuant to the Accounts and Statements Rules set out in Part I and Part IV of Chapter 9 to IPRU(INS) the Interim Prudential Sourcebook for Insurers, GENPRU the General Prudential Sourcebook and INSPRU the Prudential Sourcebook for Insurers ("the Rules") made by the Financial Services Authority under section 138 of the Financial Services and Markets Act 2000:

- Forms **[2, 3, 10 to 19, 40 to 45, 48, 49, 56, 58 and 60],** (including the supplementary notes) on pages [...] to [...] ("the Forms");

- the statement required by IPRU(INS) rule 9.29 on pages [...] to [...] ("the statement"); and

- the valuation report[s] required by IPRU(INS) rule 9.31 [(a)] on pages [...] to [...] (the valuation report[s]).

We are not required to audit and do not express an opinion on:

- Forms [46, 47, 50 to 55, 57, 59A and 59B] (including the supplementary notes) on pages [...] to [...];

- the statements required by IPRU(INS) rules 9.30 and 9.36[41] on pages [...] to [...]; and

- the certificate required by IPRU(INS) rule 9.34(1) on pages [...] to [...] .

Respective responsibilities of the insurer and its auditor

The insurer is responsible for the preparation of an annual return (including the Forms, the statement and the valuation report[s]) under the provisions of the Rules. *[The requirements of the Rules have been modified by [a] direction[s] issued under section 148 of the Financial Services and Markets Act 2000 on ....200X [and ....200X.]* Under IPRU(INS) rule 9. 11 the Forms, the statement and the valuation report[s] are required to be prepared in the manner specified by the Rules and to state fairly the information provided on the basis required by the Rules.

---

41 Required where there is a With-Profits Actuary.

The methods and assumptions determined by the insurer and used to perform the actuarial investigation as set out in the valuation report[s] are required to reflect appropriately the requirements of INSPRU 1.2 (and 1.3[42]).

It is our responsibility to form an independent opinion as to whether the Forms, the statement and the valuation report[s] meet these requirements, and to report our opinion to you. We also report to you if, in our opinion:

- adequate accounting records have not been kept, or returns adequate for our audit have not been received from branches not visited by us; or

- the Forms, the statements and the valuation report[s] are not in agreement with the accounting records and returns; or

- we have not received all the information we require for our audit.

Basis of opinion

We conducted our work in accordance with Practice Note 20 "The audit of insurers in the United Kingdom (Revised)" issued by the Auditing Practices Board. Our work included examination, on a test basis, of evidence relevant to the amounts and disclosures in the Forms, the statement and the valuation report[s]. The evidence included that previously obtained by us relating to the audit of the financial statements of the insurer for the financial year. It also included an assessment of the significant estimates and judgments made by the insurer in the preparation of the Forms, the statement and the valuation report[s].

We planned and performed our work so as to obtain all the information and explanations which we considered necessary in order to provide us with sufficient evidence to give reasonable assurance that the Forms, the statement and the valuation report[s] are free from material misstatement, whether caused by fraud or other irregularity or error and comply with IPRU(INS) rule 9.11.

In accordance with IPRU(INS) rule 9.35(1A), to the extent that any document, Form, statement, analysis or report to be examined under IPRU(INS) rule 9.35(1) contains amounts or information abstracted from the actuarial investigation performed pursuant to rule 9.4, we have obtained and paid due regard to advice from a suitably qualified actuary who is independent of the insurer.

---

42   Required for "Realistic Basis" firms only.

Opinion

In our opinion:

(i) the Forms, the statement and the valuation report[s] fairly state the information provided on the basis required by the Rules [as modified] and have been properly prepared in accordance with the provisions of those Rules; and

(ii) the methods and assumptions determined by the insurer and used to perform the actuarial investigation as set out in the valuation report[s] appropriately reflect the requirements of INSPRU 1.2 [and 1.3].

Statutory auditor   *Address*
Date

1.3 – REGULATORY REPORT: GENERAL INSURER

..............................[GENERAL INSURANCE COMPANY LIMITED]

[Global business/UK branch business]

Financial year ended 31 December 201x

Independent auditor's report to the directors pursuant to rule 9.35 of the Interim Prudential Sourcebook for Insurers ("IPRU(INS)")
We have audited the following documents prepared by the insurer pursuant to the Accounts and Statements Rules set out in Part I and Part IV of Chapter 9 to IPRU(INS) the Interim Prudential Sourcebook for Insurers, GENPRU the General Prudential Sourcebook and INSPRU the Prudential Sourcebook for Insurers ("the Rules") made by the Financial Services Authority under section 138 of the Financial Services and Markets Act 2000:

- Forms **[1, 3, 10 to 13, 15 to 17, 20A, 20 to 32, 34 and 36 to 39]**, (including the supplementary notes) on pages [...] to [...] ("the Forms"); and

- the statements required by IPRU(INS) rules 9.25, 9.26, 9.27 and 9.29 on pages [...] to [...] ("the statements").

We are not required to audit and do not express an opinion on:

- the statements required by IPRU(INS) rules 9.30, 9.32 and 9.32A on pages [...] to [...] and

- the certificate required by IPRU(INS) rule 9.34(1) on pages [...] to [...] .

Respective responsibilities of the insurer and its auditor
The insurer is responsible for the preparation of an annual return (including the Forms and the statements) under the provisions of the Rules. **[The requirements of the Rules have been modified by [a] direction[s] issued under section 148 of the Financial Services and Markets Act 2000 on ....200X [and ....200X.]** Under IPRU(INS) rule 9.11 the Forms and the statements are required to be prepared in the manner specified by the Rules and to state fairly the information provided on the basis required by the Rules.

It is our responsibility to form an independent opinion as to whether the Forms, and the statements meet these requirements, and to report our opinion to you. We also report to you if, in our opinion:

- adequate accounting records have not been kept, or returns adequate for our audit have not been received from branches not visited by us; or

- the Forms, the statements and the valuation report[s] are not in agreement with the accounting records and returns; or
- we have not received all the information we require for our audit.

Basis of opinion

We conducted our work in accordance with Practice Note 20 "The audit of insurers in the United Kingdom (Revised)" issued by the Auditing Practices Board. Our work included examination, on a test basis, of evidence relevant to the amounts and disclosures in the Forms and the statements. The evidence included that previously obtained by us relating to the audit of the financial statements of the insurer for the financial year. It also included an assessment of the significant estimates and judgments made by the insurer in the preparation of the Forms and statements.

We planned and performed out work so as to obtain all the information and explanations which we considered necessary in order to provide us with sufficient evidence to give reasonable assurance that the Forms and the statements are free from material misstatement, whether caused by fraud or other irregularity or error and comply with IPRU(INS) rule 9.11.

Opinion

In our opinion the Forms and the statements fairly state the information provided on the basis required by the Rules [as modified] and have been properly prepared in accordance with the provisions of those Rules.

Statutory auditor   *Address*
Date

1.4 – STATEMENT ON THE GROUP CAPITAL ADEQUACY REPORT

Independent auditor's statement to the directors pursuant to rule 9.40(3)(c) of the Interim Prudential Sourcebook for Insurers ("IPRU(INS)")

....

Financial year ended 31 December 201X

We have reviewed the report[43] prepared pursuant to rule 9.40(1) of IPRU(INS) on pages (x) to (x) ("the report") prepared by Example Insurance Company Ltd ("the insurer").

Respective responsibilities of the insurer and its auditors

The insurer is responsible for the preparation of the report under the provisions of rule 9.40(1) of IPRU(INS) [as modified by a direction granted under section 148 of the Financial Services and Markets Act 2000]. (The report has been prepared on the basis set out on pages [x] to[x].)

It is our responsibility to carry out the procedures set out below in the basis of opinion section, and to report whether anything of significance has come to our attention to indicate that the report has not been properly compiled in accordance with INSPRU 6.1 [as modified] and rule 9.40(1) of IPRU(INS) from information provided to the insurer by other members of the insurance group and from the insurer's own records.

Our work did not constitute an audit in accordance with International Standards on Auditing (UK and Ireland), issued by the Auditing Practices Board, of the information provided to the insurer by other members of the insurance group and included no independent examination by us of any of the underlying financial information therein. It therefore provides a lower level of assurance than an audit.

Basis of opinion

Our work consisted principally of;

- comparing on a test basis, the compilation of the report with the information provided to the insurer by other members of the insurance group and with information from the insurer's own records;

- confirming the mathematical accuracy of the compilation of the financial information contained in the report;

---

43 Where the ultimate EEA insurance parent undertaking produces consolidated accounts or publishes a capital statement in the form prescribed by FRC 27, IPRU(INS) 9.40(1A) extends the group capital adequacy report to include additional information not required to be included within the scope of the auditor's statement. Consequently the auditor's statement will need to clearly identify those parts of the group capital adequacy report within the scope of the auditor's statement.

- [reading the instructions issued to other members of the insurance group and comparing these with the requirements set out in INSPRU 6.1;] and

- comparing on a test basis, the information provided to the insurer by other members of the insurance group and any adjustments made by the insurer thereto, with:

    (a) [the instructions issued by the insurer;]

    (b) [the basis of preparation set out on pages [x] to [x]; and

    (c) the requirements set out in INSPRU 6.1 [as modified],

    to identify any significant areas where such information may not comply [therewith][with a), b) and c) above].

Opinion

On the basis of the above procedures, nothing of significance has come to our attention to indicate that the report has not been properly compiled in accordance with INSPRU 6.1 and 9.40(1) of IPRU(INS) [as modified] from information provided to the insurer by other members of the insurance group and from the insurer's own records.

Statutory auditor   *Address*
Date

1.5 – LLOYD'S SYNDICATE – PERSONAL ACCOUNTS AND SYNDICATE MAPA ACCOUNTS

Independent auditor's report to the members of syndicate XXX, the Council of Lloyd's and its auditor
We have reviewed the procedures and controls employed by [managing agent] in producing personal accounts and syndicate MAPA accounts in accordance with the Lloyd's Syndicate Accounting Byelaw.

Respective responsibilities of the Managing Agent and auditor
As described on page... the Managing Agent is responsible for the preparation of personal accounts and syndicate MAPA accounts in accordance with the Lloyd's Syndicate Accounting Byelaw. It is our responsibility to form an independent opinion, based on our review and to report our opinion to you.

Basis of opinion
Our review included such procedures as we considered necessary to evaluate whether the procedures and controls taken as a whole were operating with sufficient effectiveness to provide reasonable, but not absolute, assurance that personal accounts and syndicate MAPA accounts have been properly prepared in accordance with the Lloyd's Syndicate Accounting Byelaw and that the net results shown in personal accounts and syndicate MAPA accounts have been calculated in accordance with the applicable agency agreements.

These procedures included examination on a test basis of evidence of compliance with the procedures and controls in respect of the preparation of personal accounts and syndicate MAPA accounts. Our procedures did not necessarily include tests of transactions for any particular member or MAPA.

Inherent limitation
Procedures and controls are subject to inherent limitations and, accordingly, errors or irregularities may occur and not be detected. Such procedures cannot be proof against fraudulent collusion, especially on the part of those holding positions of authority or trust. Furthermore, this opinion relates only to those procedures and controls operated in connection with the position as at 31 December 201x, and should not be seen as providing assurance as to any future position, as changes to systems or controls may alter the validity of our opinion.

Opinion
In our opinion, the procedures and controls taken as a whole provide reasonable but not absolute assurance that:

(a) underwriting member personal accounts and syndicate MAPA accounts have been properly prepared in accordance with the Lloyd's Syndicate Accounting Byelaw; and

(b) the net results shown in underwriting member personal accounts and syndicate MAPA accounts have been calculated in accordance with the applicable agency agreements.

Statutory auditor   *Address*
Date

1.6 – EXAMPLE OF REPORT ON INTERIM NET PROFITS

External verification of interim net profits for the purposes of Stage A of the calculation in the Capital Resources Table in GENPRU 2 Annex 1R (where the detailed scope of the work undertaken is set out in the engagement letter)

Review report by the auditor to the board of directors of XYZ Limited ("the company")
In accordance with our engagement letter dated [date], a copy of which is attached as Appendix A, we have reviewed the company's statement of interim net profits for the period from [ ] to [ ] ("the interim period") as reported in the reporting statement ("the statement") attached as Appendix B and dated [date].

The statement is the responsibility of, and has been approved by, the directors of the company. Our review of the statement did not constitute an audit, and accordingly we do not express an audit opinion on the interim net profits reported therein.

Our review has been carried out having regard to rules and guidance contained in the FSA's General Prudential Sourcebook and Practice Note 20 "The Audit of Insurers in the United Kingdom (Revised)" issued by the Auditing Practices Board.

On the basis of the results of our review, nothing has come to our attention that causes us to believe that:

(a) the interim net profits as reported in the statement have not been calculated on the basis of the accounting policies adopted by the Company in drawing up its annual financial statements for the year ended [date] [except for][1];

(b) those accounting policies differ in any material respects from those required by United Kingdom Generally Accepted Accounting Practice[2]/International Financial Reporting Standards as adopted by the European Union; and

(c) the interim net profits amounting to £ [ ] as so reported are not reasonably stated.

Statutory auditor   *Address*
Date

Note 1:   Identify any changes arising from the adoption of revised accounting policies that will first be applied in the financial statements containing the interim period.

Note 2:   United Kingdom Generally Accepted Accounting Practice comprises, Schedule 3 to the 2008 Accounts and Reports Regulations, UK accounting standards and the Statement of Recommended Practice on Accounting for Insurance Business issued by the Association of British Insurers.

APPENDIX 2

THE MAIN PARTS OF FSMA 2000 RELEVANT TO INSURERS[44]

Part I (and Schedule 1) sets out matters concerning the structure and governance of the FSA including its regulatory objectives and the principles to be followed in meeting those objectives.

Part II (and Schedule 2) sets out the general prohibition on conducting regulated business unless a person (including in a corporate sense) is either authorised or exempt, including restrictions on financial promotions. Regulated activities are defined in a statutory instrument. (SI 2001/544)

Part III (and Schedules 3-5) sets out the requirements to become authorised either by receiving a specific permission from the FSA or through the EU single market rules. Exempt persons are listed in a separate statutory instrument. (SI 2001/1201)

Part IV (and Schedule 6) sets out the arrangements for application for a permission to undertake authorised business and the criteria (Threshold Conditions) that must be met. An applicant who is refused can apply to the Financial Services and Markets Tribunal (established under Part IX).

Part V sets out the provisions applying to individuals performing designated functions (controlled functions) in an authorised firm. The FSA can specify controlled functions and firms must take reasonable care to ensure that only persons approved by the FSA can undertake these functions. The FSA can specify qualification, training and competence requirements and approved persons must comply with the FSA's statement of principles and code of conduct for approved persons. Appeals can be made to the Tribunal.

Part VII allows transfers of insurance business from one insurer to another, in whole or in part, through a process of court approval.

Part VIII gives the FSA powers to impose penalties for market abuse – using information not generally available; creating a false or misleading impression; or failure to observe normal standards. Abuse is judged from the point of view of a regular market user. FSA powers extend to all persons – not only authorised persons. The FSA is required to publish a code to give guidance on what is abuse and to provide a "safe harbour". This forms part of the Market Conduct Sourcebook and is called the Code of Market Conduct.

Part X provides the FSA with general powers to make rules which apply to authorised persons, including rules on specific matters – e.g. client money, money laundering. Rules must be

---

44 Lloyd's corporate members are not subject to FSMA 2000.

published in draft for consultation. Guidance may be provided individually or generally and may be published. The FSA may modify rules or waive particular rules for particular persons in certain situations.

Part XI allows the FSA to gather information from authorised persons, including use of skilled persons' reports under section 166, or to commission investigations into authorised persons.

Part XIV sets out the disciplinary measures available to the FSA which can include public censure, unlimited fines, withdrawal of authorisation.

Part XXII includes the provisions relating to auditors and their appointment.

Part XXVI brings together in one place the arrangements applying to warning notices and decision notices concerning possible breaches of various requirements imposed by FSMA 2000 or by FSA rules. A warning notice has to state the reasons for proposed actions and allow reasonable time for representations to be made. This will be followed by a decision notice with a right to appeal to the Tribunal.

APPENDIX 3

THE FSA HANDBOOK

1. Not all authorised firms are required to comply with all rules contained within the FSA Handbook. This varies with the type of permission – the regulated activity an authorised firm is permitted to undertake is set out in the authorised firm's Scope of Permission. The following can be viewed on the FSA website:

    *   Contents of the FSA Handbook – www.fsa.gov.uk/Pages/handbook.

    *   FSA register which lists the regulated activities that each authorised firm has permission to undertake – www.fsa.gov.uk/Pages/register.

2. In gaining an understanding of the FSA Handbook the auditor bears in mind the four statutory objectives of the FSA, set out in paragraph 28 of the "Legislative and Regulatory Framework" section of this Practice Note, which underpin the content of the FSA Handbook. To facilitate usage the FSA Handbook has been structured into a number of blocks and within each block the material has been sub-divided into Sourcebooks, Manuals or Guides. There are rules, evidential provisions[45] and guidance which are contained within all of the blocks[46] Contravention of rules (which includes Principles for Businesses) or evidential provisions can give rise to an obligation on the auditor to report the matter direct to the FSA – see the section of this Practice Note relating to ISA (UK and Ireland) 250 Section B. Outline details of certain elements of the FSA Handbook are set out below.

Principles for Businesses

3. The eleven Principles for Businesses, which are general statements that set out the fundamental obligations of firms under the regulatory system, are set out in the FSA Handbook. They derive their authority from the FSA's rule-making powers as set out in the Act and reflect the regulatory objectives. These Principles are as follows:

    (1) An authorised firm must conduct its business with integrity.

    (2) An authorised firm must conduct its business with due skill, care and diligence.

    (3) An authorised firm must take reasonable care to organise and control its affairs responsibly and effectively with adequate risk management systems.

---

45 An evidential provision is not binding in its own right, but establishes a presumption of compliance or non-compliance with another rule. Guidance may be used to explain the implications of other provisions, to indicate possible means of compliance, or to recommend a particular course of action or arrangement.

46 Rules are set out in emboldened type and are marked with the icon "R", evidential provisions are marked "E" and guidance "G". Further guidance on the status of the Handbook is set out in the General Provisions (GEN) Sourcebook Chapter 2.2 and Chapter 6 of the Reader's Guide.

(4)   An authorised firm must maintain adequate financial resources.

(5)   An authorised firm must observe proper standards of market conduct.

(6)   An authorised firm must pay due regard to the interests of its customers and treat them fairly.

(7)   An authorised firm must pay due regard to the information needs of its clients, and communicate information to them in a way which is clear, fair and not misleading.

(8)   An authorised firm must manage conflicts of interest fairly, both between itself and its customers and between a customer and another client.

(9)   An authorised firm must take reasonable care to ensure the suitability of its advice and discretionary decisions for any customer who is entitled to rely on its judgment.

(10) An authorised firm must arrange adequate protection for clients' assets when it is responsible for them.

(11) An authorised firm must deal with its regulators in an open and co-operative way, and must disclose to the FSA appropriately anything relating to the firm of which the FSA would reasonably expect notice.

Senior management arrangements, systems and controls

4.   SYSC amplifies Principle for Businesses 3, the requirement for a firm to take reasonable care to organise and control its affairs responsibly and effectively, with adequate risk management systems. The relevant chapters[47], are as follows;

2 – senior management arrangements

3 – systems and controls

4 – general organisational requirements

5 – employees, agents and other relevant persons

6 – compliance, internal audit and financial crime

7 – risk control

8 – outsourcing

9 – record keeping

10 – conflicts of interest

11 – liquidity risk systems and controls

12 – group risk systems and control requirements

---

47   Chapters 13-17 apply only to insurers.

13 – operational risk

14 – prudential risk management

15 – credit risk management

16 – market risk management

17 – insurance risk

18 – guidance on Public Disclosure Act – whistle blowing

19 – remuneration code

20 – reverse stress testing

Threshold conditions

5.   Under Section 41 and Schedule 6 of FSMA 2000, the Threshold Conditions are the minimum requirements that must be met at authorisation and must continue to be met. The Threshold Conditions relevant to an insurer are:

(a) Legal status: contracts of insurance can only be effected and carried out by a body corporate (other than a limited liability partnership), a registered friendly society or a member of Lloyd's;

(b) Location of offices: the head office of a body corporate must be in the same territory/ member state as the registered office;

(c) Claims representatives: the carrying on of motor vehicle liability insurance business requires a claims representative to be appointed in each EEA State other than the UK;

(d) Close links: close links must not prevent effective supervision. Entities are regarded as closely linked if there is a group relationship, i.e. parent/subsidiary/fellow subsidiary (but using the EC 7th Company Law Directive definition of subsidiary). They are also closely linked if one owns or controls 20% or more of the voting rights or capital of the other;

(e) Adequate resources : the firm must have adequate resources (financial and non financial) for the type of business conducted taking into account the impact of other group entities and having regard to provisions made against liabilities (including contingent and future liabilities) and the approach to risk management; and

(f) Suitability: the firm must satisfy the FSA that it is fit and proper to have Part IV permission in all the circumstances. Although the emphasis is on the firm, the FSA will also consider the fitness and propriety of individuals, including whether business is conducted with integrity and in compliance with high standards and whether there is competent and prudent management and exercise of due skill, care and diligence. This will include consideration of whether those subject to the approved persons regime (i.e. those undertaking controlled functions) are, or will be, approved by the FSA.

APPENDIX 4

REPORTING DIRECT TO THE FSA – STATUTORY RIGHT AND PROTECTION FOR DISCLOSURE UNDER GENERAL LAW

1. When the auditor concludes that a matter does not give rise to a statutory duty to report direct to the FSA, the auditor considers the right to report to FSA.

2. In cases of doubt, general law provides protection for disclosing certain matters to a proper authority in the public interest.

3. Audit firms are protected from the risk of liability from breach of confidence or defamation under general law even when carrying out work which is not clearly undertaken in the capacity of auditor provided that:

    (a) In the case of breach of confidence:

        (i) Disclosure is made in the public interest; and

        (ii) Such disclosure is made to an appropriate body or person; and

        (iii) There is no malice motivating the disclosure; and

    (b) In the case of defamation:

        (i) The information disclosed was obtained in a proper capacity; and

        (ii) There is no malice motivating the disclosure.

4. The same protection is given even if there is only a reasonable suspicion that noncompliance with law or regulations has occurred. Provided that it can be demonstrated that an audit firm, in disclosing a matter in the public interest, has acted reasonably and in good faith, it would not be held by the court to be in breach of duty to the institution even if, an investigation or prosecution having occurred, it were found that there had been no breach of law or regulation.

5. When reporting to proper authorities in the public interest, it is important that, in order to retain the protection of qualified privilege, the auditor reports only to one who has a proper interest to receive the information. The FSA is the proper authority in the case of an authorised institution.

6. 'Public interest' is a concept which is not capable of general definition. Each situation must be considered individually. In general circumstances, matters to be taken into account when considering whether disclosure is justified in the public interest may include:

- The extent to which the suspected non-compliance with law or regulations is likely to affect members of the public.

- Whether the directors (or equivalent) have rectified the matter or are taking, or are likely to take, effective corrective action.

- The extent to which non-disclosure is likely to enable the suspected non-compliance with law or regulations to recur with impunity.

- The gravity of the matter.

- Whether there is a general management ethos within the insurer of disregarding law or regulations.

- The weight of evidence and the degree of the auditor's suspicion that there has been an instance of non-compliance with law or regulations.

7. Determination of where the balance of public interest lies requires careful consideration. The auditor needs to weigh the public interest in maintaining confidential client relationships against the public interest of disclosure to a proper authority and to use its professional judgment to determine whether its misgivings justify the auditor in carrying the matter further or are too insubstantial to deserve report.

8. In cases where it is uncertain whether the statutory duty requires or section 342 or section 343 FSMA 2000 permits an auditor to communicate a matter to the FSA, it is possible that the auditor may be able to rely on the defence of disclosure in the public interest if it communicates a matter to the FSA which could properly be regarded as having material significance in conformity with the guidance in ISA (UK and Ireland) 250 Section B and this Practice Note, although the auditor may wish to seek legal advice in such circumstances.

APPENDIX 5

DEFINITIONS

Abbreviations and frequently used terms in this Practice Note are set out below:

AAB	Audit Arrangements Byelaw (applicable to the Lloyd's Insurance Market).
ABI	Association of British Insurers.
Actuarial Function Holder	An Actuary appointed by an insurer carrying on long-term insurance business to perform the actuarial function.
ARROW II	"Advanced Risk Responsive Operating Framework". The term used for FSA's risk assessment process – the application of risk based supervision. It is the mechanism through which the FSA evaluates the risk an authorised firm poses to its statutory objectives enabling it to allocate its resources appropriately and respond to the risks identified. The original framework was revised and updated after its first few years of operation, with the current framework, referred to as ARROW II, being rolled out in 2006.
Auditor's expert	An individual or organization possessing expertise in a field other than accounting or auditing, whose work in that field is used by the auditor to assist the auditor in obtaining sufficient appropriate audit evidence. An auditor's expert may be either an auditor's internal expert (who is a partner or staff, including temporary staff, of the auditor's firm or a network firm), or an auditor's external expert.
Authorised firm	An insurer which has been granted one of more Part IV permissions by the FSA and so is authorised under FSMA 2000 to undertake regulated activities – an authorised person. Authorised firms include insurers other than Lloyd's corporate members.
Authorised person	Term used throughout FSMA 2000 and related statutory instruments to refer to an authorised firm – see above.
Authorised insurance company	A company registered under CA 2006 that is authorised by the FSA to conduct insurance business, together with UK branches of insurers established outside the EEA.
BAS	Board for Actuarial Standards
CA 2006	The Companies Act 2006.

Closely linked entity	As defined in section 343(8) FSMA 2000, an entity has close links with an authorised firm for this purpose if the entity is a: (a) Parent undertaking of an authorised firm; (b) Subsidiary undertaking of an authorised firm; (c) Parent undertaking of a subsidiary undertaking of an authorised firm; or (d) Subsidiary undertaking of a parent undertaking of an authorised firm.
Council of Lloyd's	The Council constituted by section 3 of Lloyd's Act 1982.
COND	Threshold conditions element of the high level standards block of the FSA Handbook.
EEA	European Economic Area.
EU-IFRSs	International Financial Reporting Standards as adopted by the European Union.
FSA	The Financial Services Authority.
FSMA 2000	The Financial Services and Markets Act 2000.
GENPRU	General Prudential Sourcebook.
IBNR	Incurred But Not Reported.
Insurance companies	The term is used, where appropriate, to refer both to authorised insurance companies and to Lloyd's corporate members.
Insurers	The term "insurers" is used in this Practice Note to refer to insurance companies authorised by the FSA (insurers with their head offices in the UK and, insurers established outside the EEA with UK branches as well as to Lloyd's Syndicates and corporate members.
Insurance SORP	The Statement of Recommended Practice "Accounting for insurance business" issued by the Association of British Insurers (ABI).
INSPRU	Prudential Sourcebook for Insurers.
IPRU(INS)	Interim Prudential Sourcebook for Insurers
JMLSG	Joint Money Laundering Steering Group
Lloyd's corporate member	A member of the Society which is a body corporate (including limited liability partnerships) or a Scottish limited partnership.

Management's expert	An individual or organisation possessing expertise in a field other than accounting or auditing, whose work in that field is used by the insurer to assist in preparing the financial statements.
MAPA	Members' Agents Pooling Arrangements.
Material significance	A matter or group of matters is normally of material significance to a regulator's function when, due either to its nature or its potential financial impact, it is likely of itself to require investigation by the regulator.
Part IV permission	A permission granted by FSA under Part IV FSMA 2000 permitting an authorised firm to carry on regulated activities as specified in the FSMA 2000 Regulated Activities Order SI 2001/544 as amended.
PPFM	Principles and Practices of Financial Management.
Principles for Businesses	FSA Handbook defined principles with which an authorised firm must comply. The 11 principles are included in a stand alone module of the high level Standards block of the FSA Handbook – PRIN.
Recognised Accountant	An accountant included on the Council of Lloyds' list of individuals and firms identified as recognised accountants. Recognised accountants are engaged either by a syndicate to perform the annual solvency audit or annual syndicate audit or by a syndicate or Lloyd's underwriting agent to act as reporting accountant.
Relevant requirement	In relation to the auditor's duty to report direct to the FSA – requirement by or under FSMA 2000 which relates to authorisation under FSMA 2000 or to the carrying on of any regulated activity. This includes not only relevant statutory instruments but also the FSA's rules (other than the Listing rules) including the Principles for Businesses. The duty to report also covers any requirement imposed by or under any other Act the contravention of which constitutes an offence which the FSA has the power to prosecute under FSMA 2000.
Reporting Accountant	An accountant appointed by a managing agent on behalf of a syndicate or an underwriting agent for the purposes of reporting to the Council pursuant to paragraph 13 of the AAB [under which the Council of Lloyd's can require a report according to a scope that it sets].
Reporting Actuary	An Actuary appointed by an insurer to report on the long-term technical provisions in the financial statements, as defined in Guidance Note 7 issued by The Institute and Faculty of Actuaries and adopted by the BAS.

Reviewing Actuary	An actuary engaged by an auditor as an "Auditor's Expert". A Reviewing Actuary is an internal auditor's expert when the actuary is a partner or staff member of the auditor's firm or a network firm. A Reviewing Actuary appointed from outside the auditor's firm is an external auditor's expert. (See section on ISA 620 (UK and Ireland) "Using the Work of an Auditor's Expert".
RITC	"reinsurance to close".
Run-off account	A syndicate year of account which has not been closed at the normal date of closure and remains open.
2001 Regulations	SI 2001/2587 – FSMA 2000 (Communications by Auditors) Regulations 2001.
2008 Regulations	SI 2008/1950 Insurance Accounts Directive (Lloyd's Syndicate and Aggregate Accounts) Regulations 2008.
2008 Accounts and Reports Regulations	SI 2008/410 The Large and Medium-sized Companies and Groups (Accounts and Reports) Regulations 2008.
2008 Lloyd's Regulations	SI 2008/1950 Insurance Accounts Directive (Lloyd's Syndicate and Aggregate Accounts) Regulations 2008.
SAO	Statement of Actuarial Opinion.
SOCA	Serious Organised Crime Agency.
Society	The Society incorporated by the Lloyd's Act 1871 by the names of Lloyd's.
SUP	Supervision manual.
SYSC	Senior management arrangements, systems and controls.
The Solvency Byelaw	The Solvency and Reporting Byelaw (No 5 of 2007) (applicable to the Lloyd's Insurance Market).
Syndicate	A group of underwriting members underwriting insurance business at Lloyd's through the agency of a managing agent.

Those charged with governance	ISAs (UK and Ireland) use the term "those charged with governance" to describe the persons entrusted with the supervision, control and direction of an entity, who will normally be responsible for the quality of financial reporting, and the term "management" to describe those persons who perform senior managerial functions. The FSA Handbook of Rules and Guidance (FSA Handbook) uses the term "governing body" to describe collectively those charged with governance. In the context of this Practice Note, references to those charged with governance includes directors of insurance companies, directors of Lloyd's managing agents, and the members of the Council of Lloyd's. Directors of Lloyd's corporate members do not fall within the scope of the FSA Handbook as regards insurance matters.
Threshold Conditions	The minimum standards that an authorised firm needs to meet to become and remain authorised by the FSA. The 6 conditions are included in a stand alone element of the high level Standards block of the FSA Handbook – COND.
UK GAAP	United Kingdom Generally Accepted Accounting Practice. This consists of applicable law, United Kingdom Accounting Standards and the Statement of Recommended Practice on Accounting for Insurance Business issued by the Association of British Insurers..
WPICC	With-Profits Insurance Capital Component.

APPENDIX 6

CROSS REFERENCES TO SIGNIFICANT TOPICS DEALT WITH IN THE PRACTICE NOTE

TOPIC	PARAGRAPH NUMBER	SECTION
Considerations relating to Lloyds	15-19 22-26 35 46-47 52 and 59 66, 69 and 71-72 88 and 104-121 128-129 151-153 182 213-219 230 232-233 239-241 256-265 318-328 Appendix 1.5	Legislative and Regulatory Framework Financial statements Reporting direct to the FSA ISA (UK and Ireland) 210 ISA (UK and Ireland) 240 ISA (UK and Ireland) 250 (Section A) ISA (UK and Ireland) 250 (Section B) ISA (UK and Ireland) 300 ISA (UK and Ireland) 315 ISA (UK and Ireland) 402 ISA (UK and Ireland) 540 ISA (UK and Ireland) 560 ISA (UK and Ireland) 570 ISA (UK and Ireland) 600 ISA (UK and Ireland) 700 Reporting on regulatory returns Illustrative example auditor's reports
Statutory equalisation provisions	249-255 269	ISA (UK and Ireland) 700 ISA (UK and Ireland) 705
Group capital adequacy report	2 329-337 Appendix 1.4	Introduction Reporting on Regulatory Returns Illustrative example auditor's report
Report on interim net profits	338-342 Appendix 1.6	Reporting on Regulatory Returns Illustrative example auditor's report
Right and duty to report direct to the FSA	2 77-121 Appendix 4	Introduction ISA (UK and Ireland) 250 Section B Reporting direct to the FSA

Technical provisions	21	Introduction
	122, 124-126	ISA (UK and Ireland) 300
	132, 143-144, 148	ISA (UK and Ireland) 315
	158	ISA (UK and Ireland) 320
	163, 178	ISA (UK and Ireland) 330
	183, 185	ISA (UK and Ireland) 450
	196-221	ISA (UK and Ireland) 540
	235	ISA (UK and Ireland) 580
	242-248	ISA (UK and Ireland) 620
	251	ISA (UK and Ireland) 700
	267	ISA (UK and Ireland) 705
	270-272	ISA (UK and Ireland) 706
	314, 326, 342	Regulatory returns
Use of actuaries	21	Introduction
	50	ISA (UK and Ireland) 230
	197-205	ISA (UK and Ireland) 540
	242-248	ISA (UK and Ireland) 620
	293-309	Regulatory returns

**THE AUDITING
PRACTICES BOARD**